The Sustainable Soul

The Sustainable Soul

Eco-Spiritual Reflections and Practices

Rebecca James Hecking

Skinner House Books
Boston

Printed in the United States

Cover and text design by Suzanne Morgan

print ISBN: 978-1-55896-605-5
eBook ISBN: 978-1-55896-608-6

6 5 4 3 2
23

Library of Congress Cataloging-in-Publication Data

Hecking, Rebecca James.
  The sustainable soul : eco-spiritual reflections and practices /
Rebecca James Hecking.

     p. cm.
  ISBN-13: 978-1-55896-605-5 (pbk. : alk. paper)
  ISBN-10: 1-55896-606-4 (pbk. : alk. paper)
  ISBN-13: 978-1-55896-608-6 (ebook)
  1. Human ecology—Religious aspects. 2. Spirituality. I. Title.
  GF80.H435 2011
  201'.77—dc22
                              2010041644

To my children:

Steven

Matthew

Julia

With hope for the healing and restoration
of the Earth your generation will inherit.

And love. Always love.

Contents

Introduction

Tucked in among the many legends of King Arthur and his court is the story of the Fisher King. The Fisher King is an enigmatic character, but one that holds profound meaning for us today. He bore a wound that would not heal, and his personal health was tied to the condition of his kingdom. As a result of his personal wound, his kingdom had become a wasteland, unable to heal until he himself found healing and restoration. The health of the king and the health of the land were inextricably intertwined. In the end, both the king and the land were restored.

Modern society, and we who live in it are psychological kin to the mythic Fisher King. We as a species preside over the growing wasteland that our planet will become if we continue on our present trajectory. And yet, collectively, we go about our daily lives oblivious to this truth. This book intends to pose the questions that can heal us. We are wounded in our collective psyche, conditioned by centuries of living out of touch with the natural world. Until we begin to ask the right questions and make the deeper connections, both we and our world will continue to suffer a wound that will not heal. Each chapter in this book asks you to examine a particular aspect of your attitudes to, beliefs about, and connections with the natural world. It then offers questions and spiritual practices to help you take these explorations deeper and find out what's true for you personally. Whether you're reading this book on your own or as part of a group, I hope you will find some healing and restoration.

Like so many people, I am deeply concerned about the future of the Earth. I worry about how the next few decades will play out, especially since it seems that, globally, we are losing ground on nearly every environmental problem faced by humanity. Another species gone here, another toxic spill there, as the clock of irreversible climate change keeps ticking. Meanwhile, day-to-day life persists and we carry on, mostly unconscious about these ominous developments. I have gradually come to realize that the foundational problem underlying all environmental issues of our day is a spiritual one. What humanity needs is not another "Let's go green" campaign, complete with free T-shirts, but rather a deep, seismic shift in how we see the Earth, and how we see ourselves in relation to it. We desperately need, on a global scale, an infusion into our collective consciousness of a sense of the same spiritual connection that I experienced—that we've all experienced at some point—outdoors as a child. It is that gut-level sense of the Sacred all around us, permeating every branch, leaf, and stone. We need to re-sanctify the biosphere and remember the knowledge that rests deep in our bones: that we are the Earth, the Earth is us, and that this literal ground that is the source of our being is completely holy. Most importantly, we need to consciously bring this spiritual connection into our daily lives, allowing it to inform our everyday experience and choices.

This understanding has the power to transcend barriers of culture, place, politics, and, to some extent, religion. It is a human thing, a resident-of-the-Earth thing, flowing underneath and around the barriers that divide us, like water around rocks in a stream. If you are a committed member of an established religion, the ideas presented here can be adapted and integrated into your own framework of beliefs. If you are an avowed atheist, this is fine too. No particular beliefs are needed; simply being a resident of the Earth is enough. If you are a seeker, then explore to your heart's content. Find what speaks to you and resonates with your spirit—and don't get stuck on what doesn't.

I take as my starting point the direct experience of the natural world, and inform that with understanding gleaned from science. Today, we possess scientific knowledge unimaginable to previous generations, and that knowledge is growing at an exponential rate. If we choose to embrace it, this knowledge can become a contemporary mythos for us. I do not mean *myth* in the sense of something false, but rather a sacred story that offers insight into our lived experience. It is a mistake to ignore science—leaving it to folks in white lab coats, and not engaging with it ethically and spiritually—since science has provided the knowledge that led us down the path of ecological destruction. Science without spirit is toxic to us and the rest of the natural world, and we have seen the tangible outcomes of this in the past century. On the other hand, science informed by an ethical spirituality, grounded in the sacredness of the natural world, can be a force for healing and restoring our world.

Spirituality that has the potential to cross religious and cultural boundaries, as well as contribute to the healing and restoration of the Earth, is not only an intellectual exercise. Abstract philosophical discussion is lovely, particularly when experienced in the company of friends over dinner and a bottle of good wine, but alone it is not enough. Direct experience—our starting point—needs to be an ongoing part of our daily lives. We must ask ourselves: How do we spend our days? Do we pause and connect with the natural world, drawing sustenance and solace for life's challenges? Or do we remain isolated and oblivious to the biosphere that enables us to live?

The practices in each chapter of this book are designed to bring this natural form of spirituality out of the fuzzy philosophical ether and into the realm of the ordinary. Whether the practice involves playing with ideas in visualization, taking a mindful walk, or writing a journal entry, the idea is the same: to engage with the natural world on a deeper level. When you do this on a regular basis, you will find that the Earth becomes a kind of a presence in your life. For example, if you're having a tough day, you may find yourself drawn to step outside and breathe deeply while watching the birds—something you never did before, but that somehow just feels right. Or you may find yourself asking questions about our society's priorities in new and different ways. You might begin to notice details of the natural world all around: trees budding in the spring, shifts in the breeze, or the slow seasonal dance of changing constellations in the sky.

No matter how it happens in your individual life, the common experience for all of us is the sense of coming home to the Earth, and to a way of being that is more deeply and truly human. Our kind has walked the Earth for approximately half a million years, but the plastic-coated, computer-driven, hyper-industrialized, nuclear-powered, Anthropocene age is only a tiny fraction (.0012 percent) of this. Even what we call civilization has only been around for 2 percent of our time here. For approximately 98 percent of our existence, we lived in close communion with the natural world. Without romanticizing this time, we should acknowledge that while much has been gained in the process of becoming "civilized," we have also suffered tremendous losses that we are only now beginning to comprehend. We have forgotten who we are. It is as though we have fractured something deep within. Like the wounded Fisher King, who presided over a wasteland, the injuries to our collective psyche are reflected in the injuries to the Earth. As we heal ourselves and reconnect with the natural world, we will also see the Earth beginning a journey of restoration. The task now is to rediscover and reclaim our lost legacy, and begin the healing process.

Welcome home.

How to Use This Book

Short answer: any way you want. This book is designed to be interactive. As such, you and I are collaborators. My goal is to offer a transformative vision of the entire Earth as sacred space. I hope that after reading the book and working through the exercises, you will integrate some form of natural spirituality into your life. I am not trying to convert you to anything, but rather to offer concepts and ideas that will enrich your spiritual path, whatever it may be. If a practice feels uncomfortable, stop and ask yourself: Is my reaction due to being stretched from my comfort zone? If so, then persevere. On the other hand, if a practice contradicts your deeply held religious beliefs, then pick something else that better suits your particular path. Try to work through at least one practice per chapter, but if this is not possible, be sure to spend some time thinking through the questions at the end of each chapter. Take your time. Allow some breathing room for your own thoughts and feelings to develop.

The book is written for group or individual use. Each chapter offers several practices that can easily be adapted for use in a variety of situations.

There is also one practice per chapter that is designed especially for groups of twelve or more. At the end of each chapter, you'll also find questions suitable for group discussion. Of course, these can also be used by individuals for reflection or journaling.

Groups can use the book in several ways, as listed below. Choose one that best suits the unique personality of your group and its members, or create something new. For more information on large groups, see "Tips for Group Facilitators" (page 157).

~ For a discussion group that meets on a regular basis, individuals can read the chapters and do some practices alone, then share their insights with the group.

~ Larger groups can divide into pairs or triads for doing the practices, then return and share with the group.

~ Some practices adapt easily to a large-group format. Altar work does this particularly well, and with a little advance planning, it can also be integrated into part of a worship service or retreat.

~ A group can use the themes of the four parts of this book to create a powerful and transformative weekend retreat. Select topics and practices from part one for a Friday night session, use parts two and three for Saturday, and end with part four on Sunday. This takes participants through the entire descent/transformation/renewal process (described in chapter one) in a relatively short time. If you are interested in having the author lead a retreat for your group, contact her at rebeccahecking@earthlink.net.

There are several ways to approach this book:

~ You can read straight through, working with two chapters per month.

Reading this way would take a year. One good starting time is the beginning of the calendar year. Another is autumn—this synchronizes nicely with the themes of the book. As the Earth turns toward the light, you move into the brighter territory of parts two, three, and four. This is perhaps the most difficult way to work through the book, and although it may be challenging, it could prove to be a catalyst for powerful transformation and deep spiritual growth and is highly recommended. Beginning in the summer would put you at chapter twelve at darkest winter, which is also very seasonally appropriate and an excellent way to approach the material. Of course, these are only suggestions—start at any time that feels right to you. You may choose to read through the book once before trying any practices, and this is a good idea. Having a road map in your head from pre-reading will help you navigate the journey.

᷈   You can cycle through each section monthly. This means that in a given month, you would work through one chapter per week from each section. For example, you would start with chapter one, and then go on to chapters seven, thirteen, and nineteen, before cycling back to chapter two the following month. This way of reading and working allows you to experience major themes on a more compacted timescale and has an entirely different rhythm than working straight through. It allows you to revisit your thoughts from earlier chapters within each section frequently. This method would take approximately six months to complete. You may find that you need to skim through chapters you've read previously if they are referred to in your present chapter and it's been a while since you first read them.

᷈   You can also dip into any section as your intuition dictates. If you choose to work this way, I suggest that you read the entire book straight through once (without necessarily doing the practices), since some chapters reference earlier material. Then, you can listen to your own inner voice about what section or chapter is best for you at any given time. For example, if you are experiencing a deep personal loss (a death or divorce perhaps), you may choose to focus on more joyful chapters as a way to balance yourself. On the other hand, if your spiritual life has seemed a little fluffy lately, you might choose to engage with one of the more challenging or weighty chapters. Follow your heart and all will be well.

It is also helpful to revisit chapters after some time has passed, and consider them again. Often, new insights are found after the initial experiences have time to incubate in your psyche.

As you read through each chapter, you may notice that the practices vary considerably. This is by design. I do not expect that an individual or group will do every practice completely. Some of them will resonate with you, others will not. Work within your own real-life environment and daily life. If you travel, take the book along and try a practice that might not work so well on your home turf.

I also encourage you to explore on your own. Use the chapters as a springboard for your own creativity. Adapt them to your own religious tradition. As my reader/collaborator, I expect nothing less of you. I wish you a blessed journey as we walk the sacred Earth together. We are all standing on holy ground.

A Few Notes on Altar Work

A type of practice that appears frequently in this book—altar work—may be unfamiliar to some readers. Designing and working with a small home altar can be a helpful spiritual discipline for many people, particularly those who have the impulse to create with their hands. Working with an altar does not mean worshiping the objects sitting upon it. Rather, an altar creates a designated sacred space within the home for contemplation. The objects placed on the altar serve as a focal point for contemplative thought or prayer, and provide a physical place for creative spiritual expression.

You can create an altar in all kinds of places. Many people use a small shelf or table in a private area of the home, such as a bedroom. Altars may also be located in a more public area, such as a living room or entryway. It may be possible to have an altar at your office or workplace. Altars in public spaces can serve as spiritual touchstones, calling the creator to spiritual reflection even in the midst of busy daily life—they have a different feel than altars in more private spaces. It's easy to create an altar that doesn't look overtly religious but which still carries deep spiritual meaning. Some people create altars outdoors, either on the ground or on a table, stone, or tree stump. These can be temporary or permanent installations. Many people find that it's helpful to have two altars, one that changes with the seasons or with the moods of the creator, and another that is more permanent and reflects the individual's spiritual beliefs. Needless to say, there are no limits. An altar is defined by the conscious intention of its creator.

Place on your altar whatever objects speak to you; there are no rules. Common items include candles, stones, leaves, flowers, family heirlooms, or artwork of various sorts. Objects related to your religious heritage or practices are obvious choices. Altar work as suggested in the practices provides a place for tangible expression of the essence of key concepts in the chapter. As always, these are only suggestions that can spark your own creativity. Integrate your own ideas and intuition for an altar that is uniquely yours.

Altar work can also be an excellent creative practice for groups in both formal and informal settings. A group that meets regularly in a suitable space may choose to have a permanent altar that changes and evolves as the group works through various practices. Or a temporary altar can serve as the focal point for group contemplation or meditation for a short time. Group altar work usually requires a little advance planning, but this need not be complicated. For example, to create the altar contrasting natural and artificial, described in chapter two (page 11), the group facilitator might bring a cloth to help define the altar space and have participants bring one natural object and one synthetic one. The group could create and then re-create the altar over the course of an hour or two rather than days as described in the chapter, allowing time for some reflection and discussion at the end of the practice. The creative art exercises throughout the book also lend themselves well to group altar work. As always, adapt the practices to your particular situation.

The Path of Awakening

Awakening is a challenging path. We who live in the industrialized West may find it uncomfortable to face the painful reality of the damage our culture has inflicted upon other people and the Earth itself, as well as dysfunctional aspects of our culture such as consumerism. We may even feel guilty and ashamed. Nevertheless, it is critical that we walk this path since its truth is often glossed over and ignored in favor of business as usual. To continue with things as they are is a recipe for global suffering, destruction, and death. Sooner or later, our culture will change. The only question is whether we will change voluntarily and preserve a livable Earth for future generations, or keep our blinders firmly in place and ensure catastrophic ecological collapse in the lifetimes of our children and grandchildren.

The exercises in part one are designed to offer fresh perspectives. If you're reading this book, you're probably already aware of many of the environmental problems presented here. If so, the exercises will help you to see familiar concerns in new and different ways. You may generate new ideas for discussing these issues with others, or discover spiritual insights that will enrich your own path. If you are working with a group, you may find the perspectives of your fellow group members to be enlightening and enriching as well. Blessings.

ONE

Beginning with Love

In his masterwork *The Hero with a Thousand Faces*, renowned mythologist Joseph Campbell describes the hero's journey as a process of leaving the normal world behind, journeying into a symbolic wilderness or underworld, confronting the demons or monsters that reside there, and then returning victorious with wisdom to share with others. You are embarking on such a journey. The monsters you will confront are very real. Facing the reality of the state of the natural world is daunting. Leaving behind the mindless consumerism that passes for genuine culture in our day and age, you may feel as though you are quite alone in the wilderness without ever leaving home. You will be transformed and changed in ways you might not be able to imagine here at the beginning.

You will also find joy in unexpected places, and discover that you are a member of Earth's family in ways you might never have realized. You will find that you are a part of a larger community of heroes and heroines who dare to imagine and create a different sort of world. You will claim your birthright as a being who embodies the consciousness of the planet, and embrace your part in healing the Earth.

The chapters ahead roughly parallel Campbell's concept of a hero's journey. In part one, we separate ourselves from the paradigms of the everyday world, and confront the hidden realities of business as usual. In part two, we shed the dysfunctional mindsets that keep us trapped. Like the ancient Babylonian goddess Inanna, who shed the trappings of her power and status as she journeyed to the underworld, we too will let go of the illusory ideas that keep us bound to an unsustainable cultural paradigm. We move to the depths, and in so doing we break free. Part three finds us at a turning point. Here, we have confronted the demons and lived to tell the tale. We find ourselves on the cusp of transformation, ripe for rebirth, and begin to ground ourselves in the deep wisdom of the Earth. Finally, in part four, we emerge with a new vision, ready to recreate our culture from the inside out.

Now it's time to begin. These first exercises are designed to create a little psychological space for the inward journey to come. They are ways to honor your own process and bless your own story. Choose one (or more) and make a beginning. You are embarking on a hero's journey of the spirit. Give yourself a hero's sendoff. I wish you a rich and rewarding experience, and send you off with a cheer. Huzzah!

Practices

Start a journal If you are the type of person who keeps a journal, now is a good time to start a new one. Throughout the book, you will find many journaling prompts and questions for reflection. When you're ready, make your first entry by taking a look at your world at this moment in time. Go outside. Make a note of the calendar date, day of the week, and time of day. Observe the world around you. What is the weather like? What flowers are in bloom? From which direction is the wind blowing? Do you see any birds?

Insects? Write it all down. Sketch a little, if you're so inclined. Capture this moment, right here and right now, at the beginning. Check in with yourself, and reflect on your feelings about the path ahead.

A Mindful Walk Step outside your front door. Take a deep breath. Now go. Walk at least fifteen minutes away, and then back again. This is not an exercise walk. Don't go at a fast clip. Don't disconnect by listening to music. Take the world as it is. Meander. Walk at a slow to moderate pace, and actively observe the world around you. What do you see? What do you hear? How much of what you sense is natural, and how much is human-made? Do you like all you see? If you could change part of it, what would you change? Think, observe, and walk. When you arrive home again, take another deep breath and come back into your normal world.

An Opening Ceremony Mark this beginning in some small but significant way by creating a meaningful and unique ceremony. Offer a prayer. Recite a poem aloud. Make a small offering out in the world. A handful of birdseed laid at the foot of a tree could represent a gift to the Earth. A small bouquet of flowers tossed into a stream could symbolize the beginning of your spiritual journey. What resonates with your soul?. Keep it simple, and make it personal. Perhaps write about it when you're done.

Large Group—Symbolic Action Grab some trash bags and head out to a public area that could use a little TLC. Maybe it's a neighborhood in your town with abandoned houses. Maybe it's a park that's seen better days. Don't make a big deal of it; just go. Pick up litter for an hour, and then come back to your meeting place and have some refreshments. Finally, come together as a group. Hold hands. Offer a prayer or a wish for a healed and restored

Earth. Each participant can share her own wish such as, "I wish the oceans overflowed with fish again," or "I wish more trees would be planted for those that have been cut down." Don't force participation from shy members; just keep the prayers or wishes flowing. Wrap it all up with one big group wish or closing blessing.

For Reflection

∾ What does the word *environmentalism* mean to you? Does it have positive or negative connotations? Or both? How about the word *Earth*? Do the meanings vary a lot among the group members?

∾ Read the "How to Use This Book" section (page xv). How do you want to approach the book? Do you need a plan? Do you prefer to be spontaneous? If you are working with a group, decide on a loose schedule, realizing that you may modify it as you go.

∾ Read the "A Few Notes on Altar Work" section (page xviii). What's your reaction to altar work? Is it something you might like to try? Does it make you uncomfortable, or excite your creativity? Why do you think you respond the way you do?

∾ When in your life have you experienced an opening ceremony of any sort? What was it like? How does this compare to your previous experience?

TWO

Facing Ecological Reality

Nearby my home is a discount supermarket. It's a boxy thing with a big parking lot, and it looks pretty much like thousands of others of its kind. It sells all sorts of discounted foods, processed and shipped from unknown far away factories, along with selected cheap toys, clothes, and household gadgets mostly from China. It sits next to what used to be a pond-like reservoir for a now-defunct water treatment plant. The plant was far too small to handle the needs of the town as it grew, and it was abandoned to the elements, leaving the pond behind. Across from the reservoir used to sit a century-old farmhouse, a relic from the days when the surrounding area was covered with wheat and oats instead of asphalt and concrete.

Before the supermarket was built, a small grassy field occupied the corner across from the farmhouse. Back then, if you stood facing away from the road and looked toward the pond, the area seemed almost untouched. Trees that surrounded the pond shielded the farmhouse from sight. It was a tiny slice of wildish earth at the edge of town. When my children were little, we discovered a family of geese that returned to that field near the pond every year to build a nest and raise a brood of goslings. We delighted in seeing the fuzzy babies grow into awkward half-feathered youths, then eventually fly away for another season. Obviously, the geese found sustenance and safety near the pond, and they were not disturbed by the traffic on the road nearby.

One day, all that changed. Bulldozers moved in and began to clear the ground for the supermarket to be built. They tore down the farmhouse and dug up the field. They ripped out the trees and paved over the grass. We never saw the geese again. Today, the pond is littered with trash, and all that's left of the field are a few scraggly weeds tough enough to survive a regular diet of exhaust fumes and road salt. My children and I were saddened by the loss. It seems trivial to become emotional about the demise of a few trees, a patch of grass and a few common birds, but the loss is symbolic of a thousand similar losses across the countryside, and millions of losses around the world. Those geese didn't stand a chance. The saddest irony of all is that less than a quarter mile down the main road stands an empty building that formerly housed a supermarket.

The story of the geese and their field is really the Earth's story played out in miniature. Humans have impacted the global environment in the past century in ways unprecedented in the history of the world. Environmentalist Bill McKibben points out that, in a very real sense, we have brought about the end of the natural world because we exercise god-like power to interfere with the natural systems that support us. As a culture we remain mostly oblivious to this fact. It has become almost a cliché to say that we are destroying the planet. But after hearing this phrase yet again, the daily obligations of our lives kick in, and we set aside the latest doom-and-gloom report and go to work, cook our dinner, and walk the dog. Later on, we turn on our TV sets and see commercials from companies touting how eco-friendly they are. No worries. "They" will surely solve the problem. The cliché becomes background noise amid our busy lives, and the true magnitude and severity of the issues facing us never really sink in. Whether we realize it or not, things have changed.

I subscribe to several environmental news services, from which I get regular emails. Every day, I am met with a barrage of information that *should* provoke major changes in human behavior worldwide. The climate news is particularly disturbing. Environmental writer Derrick Jensen puts it especially bluntly when he says, "Industrial civilization is killing the planet." These are harsh words, but we need to hear them. The possibility that civilization itself may fall or that the Earth may be uninhabitable for our great-grandchildren is shocking and terrifying. Read that sentence again. And a third time, slowly. Let it sink in. Allow the possibility of a ruined Earth to enter your consciousness. Imagine the human suffering between now and then if that future unfolds over the coming decades. We are consuming resources faster than the Earth can renew them, and poisoning the planet in the process. Consider the so-called Fertile Crescent, the land where civilization as we know it began. Today, it is mostly desert, incapable of sustaining its population without resources imported from elsewhere. Consider vast ocean dead zones, melting glaciers, and clear-cut forests. Jensen writes, "This way of living—industrial civilization—is based on, requires, and would collapse very quickly without persistent and widespread exploitation and degradation. This includes exploitation and degradation of the natural world." Until very recently, we could walk away from this degradation and move on to the next place to exploit, the next virgin wilderness.

It sounds strange, but the problem with most environmental crises is that unlike the small microcosm of the geese and their field, these crises tend to be either invisible to us personally (we can't see ocean species die off from our beach chairs), distant (the rainforest and the arctic are awfully far away), or on such a scale that they are incomprehensible (toxic radioactive waste will contaminate the earth for millions of years). Humanity has evolved to interact in relatively small groups within our local environment. Technology has not changed that evolutionary fact. We connect much more with individual human interest stories (and cute goslings) than with abstract scientific reports and graphs. If a TV network suddenly decided to report on ecological reality, it would quickly lose its audience as people changed the channel and slipped back into comfortable denial. On top of that, the nature of scientific inquiry isn't black and white. It's complicated and messy, and only those with a high level of technical expertise can fully understand it. For the average non-scientist, these shades of grey quickly muddle the issues beyond comprehension. From there, the slip into denial is quick and easy. No worries. They (those smart folks in lab coats) are studying the situation. Everything will be okay. Or not.

The first big step on the spiritual journey ahead is to come face to face with the truth of the ecological problems we now face as a species. When we do this, our priorities shift and our perspective changes, but it can be a painful process. Just as the loss of a single field caused my children to grieve, when we fully grasp what we as a species have done to our only home it can be heart-wrenching. In fact, if you are *not* crying a few tears or losing some sleep over these issues then you haven't truly faced them.

In the end, this is an issue of opening our hearts. Stepping out of denial, we are vulnerable. We are tender, open. Exposed. We find ourselves mourning the loss of a single tree. We grieve for the goslings, the rainforests, the oceans, and the species on the edge of extinction. We grieve the Earth and for ourselves.

Practices

Earth's Story in Miniature Find a place in your area like the paved-over field and polluted pond described above. It should be somewhere that used to be some wild territory but has now been destroyed to make way for something that humans have deemed more desirable. Spend some time observing how things are now. Then, in your journal, describe in words or with a drawing how the place used to be. Use your memories to guide you. What gifts did the place offer to humans and non-humans before it was transformed? What value did it have that cannot be expressed in dollars?

Parking Lot Meditation Drive to a shopping center during business hours, then park somewhere near the edge of the lot, facing the center. Spend at least ten minutes simply observing. Note people's comings and goings. Look at the vehicles driving in and out. After that time, close your eyes and imagine the land as it was before humans existed. What would it look like? Take your time, and allow your thoughts to vividly form a picture of the pre-human era. After a while, open your eyes. Spend another ten minutes observing; this time hold your imaginings of the pre-human era and the current reality together in your mind. Reflect on how these two images interact.

From Nature to Machine Decorate your altar with objects from nature such as stones, shells, bark, acorns, leaves, driftwood, or found feathers. Over the course of a week, remove one object at a time and replace it with an object from the modern world such as a plastic bottle, a piece of paper, an MP3 player, a cell phone, car keys, or a DVD. Reflect on the change as it occurs, either mentally or in writing. How has the sense of sacred space changed with the replacement of each item?

Large Group—Name Your Fears This exercise encourages participants to look at fears squarely and acknowledge them. Gather in a large circle. Allow time for each person to name at least one fear about the future related to ecological issues. Think not only of your fears for all of humanity but your personal fears as well. What do you fear for yourself? Your family? Your children? Your pets? Be as specific as possible. You can choose to speak in order or randomly. After each person speaks, the group should respond with the phrase "We acknowledge your fear," or a similar one of your own creation. Continue for fifteen to twenty minutes. At the end, the leader should offer an appropriate closing, acknowledging the fears of the whole group. Next, sit together in silence for five to ten minutes before ending the session.

For Reflection

∿ How has the world changed since you were a child? Think of the place where you grew up. Is it cleaner or dirtier now? Have humans encroached on previously wild land?

∿ Think of the weather patterns in the place where you grew up. Remember things such as snowfall, intensity of storms, or amount of rain. Has anything changed? If so, how is it different? Are the changes consistent with predictions about climate change for your area? Ask older people in particular for their input on this question.

∿ Have you ever heard a news story about the environment that scared you? What was it, and why was it frightening? Is it something that still concerns you today?

∿ If the Earth itself could speak to us, what would it say?

THREE

Mindless Living

Addiction. It's a word we all know too well. Chances are you know someone who has struggled with a serious addiction of some sort. We're all addicted to some degree. Whether it's to something relatively benign like coffee or something far more insidious and destructive like drugs or alcohol, the addict's mindset is a familiar one. Denial, blame, struggle . . . recovery? Denial itself can be a healthy coping mechanism when one is confronted with overwhelming trauma. With addiction, however, the trauma becomes internalized and denial is both chronic and toxic. Author Chellis Glendinning says that humanity's original trauma was the separation from the natural world that occurred with our transition from a hunter-gatherer lifestyle to a more agrarian one. In her book *My Name is Chellis and I'm in Recovery from Western Civilization*, she writes,

> The small-scale, nomadic life that had endured through more than a million years and thirty-five thousand generations was irreparably altered. The human relationship with the natural world was gradu-

ally changed from one of respect for and participation in its elliptical wholeness to one of detachment, management, control, and finally domination. The social, cultural, and ecological foundations that had previously served the development of a healthy primal matrix were undermined, and the human psyche came to develop and maintain itself in a state of chronic traumatic stress.

With such chronic stress internalized by denial, the addiction process was almost inevitable.

Looking at Western industrialized culture as a whole, it's easy to see the addiction dynamic at work in a variety of contexts. As a people, we are collectively addicted to consumerism and the maintenance of our lifestyle. Even if we personally do not have the means to live lavishly, we are still affected by the cultural mindset that declares that lifestyle a desirable one. We are addicted to petroleum, as politicians of all stripes regularly remind us (while failing to seriously address the problem). Following from these are many other cultural addictions—we're addicted to junk food, quick fixes, big cars, bigger houses, easy credit, throw-away products, and overspending.

Most active addicts simply refuse to face their problem, and find a million excuses to explain away their behavior, as well as its effects on those around them. Looking at our cultural addictions, we can see plenty of evidence of this kind of denial. Even as Pacific islands sink under rising seas and droughts, and storms and floods increase in intensity and frequency, we ignore the consequences of global climate change and engage in political posturing instead. Even as fish populations collapse and ocean garbage patches grow ever larger, we continue to overfish and pollute the seas. Even as cancer rates rise and children suffer from asthma in increasing numbers, we refuse to hold corporations responsible for the damage they inflict on the environment. We explain all of this away because we don't want to risk damaging the economy by facing the truth. We shut our eyes, cover our ears, and adopt a "la-la-la-I-can't-hear-you" attitude that allows our elected leaders to ignore reality and maintain business as usual.

Living in denial is mindless living. Thoreau perfectly described the condition when he wrote, "Most men live lives of quiet desperation." We who live in a dysfunctional addictive culture remain disconnected, out of touch, and in a state of mindless denial. This is all of us, to some extent. The path to recovery for an addict usually begins with the hitting rock bottom and/ or being confronted by loving friends in an intervention. What constitutes rock bottom varies considerably from person to person. As a culture, I don't think we're quite there yet, but frankly it's a place I don't want to go. Rock bottom would mean an utterly devastated and ravaged Earth, with unimaginable suffering for billions of people. We need an intervention instead.

The first step of the wonderfully successful twelve-step programs is for the addict to admit the problem and to admit powerlessness over the situation. In other words, it means facing up to reality. Addictions are a huge challenge, but every day across the country, someone steps forward and admits a problem. Every day, people of all walks of life successfully live another day in recovery. Just ask a recovering alcoholic. Life in recovery is so much better than the quiet desperation of addiction.

Practices

Step 8 and Beyond In twelve-step programs, the eighth and ninth step involve the addict making a list of those he has harmed and making restitution to the wronged parties as much as possible. Consider one aspect of your lifestyle—such as food, energy, or clothing—and list possible ecological and social harms that may have resulted from it. When you do this, realize that many systems related to lifestyle really are beyond our immediate control and influence. Make the list anyway. Brainstorm ways to begin to heal the damage and then follow through on the most practical of the possibilities. If you keep a journal, use it for this practice. If not, put the brainstormed ideas in a place where you will encounter them in a few weeks or months—perhaps in a file. Revisit your work, and check your progress.

Seeing with New Eyes Go out to your favorite natural spot. This can be a park or wild area, but it should be a place where you will be undisturbed. While there, sit and simply observe the natural world around you while using Chellis Glendinning's words as a mantra. She describes the traumatic change in humanity's relationship with the natural world as "detachment, management, control, domination." Repeat these words to yourself, and allow them to sink into your mind as you simply observe the natural world around you. After several minutes, pause and consider your emotional reaction to her words spoken in natural surroundings. How do you feel? What emotions does the experience evoke in you? Later, repeat the meditation in a more urban setting. Reflect on the contrast.

Stream of Consciousness Consider the following, and then write on the topic for at least ten minutes (set a timer). Move your pen continuously on the paper. Don't worry about grammar or spelling. Just write. Consider Thoreau's phrase "lives of quiet desperation." What meaning does it have for you? Have you ever known anyone to whom it would apply? Would it apply to you? How do mindless living and denial contribute to desperation?

Large Group—Experiment in Awareness Gather the group, and get on your feet. Put on some upbeat music, and walk or dance around the room for about five minutes. Be sure to move with intensity and use the entire space. Then do the same thing again; only this time have everyone walk or dance backward. Again, use the entire space and continue for about five minutes. Afterward, grab a seat and consider the following: How did the experiences differ? Did the backward movement require more mindfulness? If so, how? What can this simple, silly game teach us about breaking out of patterns of addictive, mindless living and denial in our culture? Brainstorm ways that we can use behavioral changes to snap us out of our mindless denial paradigm.

For Reflection

∿   Do you know anyone who has struggled with addiction? What has the experience of the addict and her family taught you that might be relevant to our collective cultural addictions?

∿   Can you recall any time in your life when you lived mindlessly? Think about it for a while. Does it offer you any hidden wisdom?

∿   Can you recall any experiences of heightened awareness? Were these brief or extended? How does this type of experience differ from the practice of living mindfully?

∿   What does the word *denial* mean to you personally? Now, make the question bigger: What does the word *denial* mean to all of us collectively? How does denial play out in our culture?

FOUR

How Much Is Enough?

Not long ago, my family had an old clunker of a car that we jokingly referred to as "the rust bucket," or sometimes just "the bucket" for short. It was a small second car that got good gas mileage and was used mostly for short trips, but it was about fifteen years old and looked its age. During the last few years of its life, before it made that final journey to the junkyard, it had gotten so awful looking that our kids were embarrassed to be seen riding in it. If they needed to go somewhere, they would beg for us to take the mini-van instead. Mostly we acquiesced, but occasionally the kids were forced to ride in the bucket, much to their dismay.

My personal concerns about the bucket centered mostly on its potential to break down at inopportune times, but I confess that there were moments when I felt a little twinge of what my kids expressed so openly and honestly. A small, deep-down part of me wanted to hang a large sign on the bucket that read something like, "We're trying to save the earth's resources!" My feelings about the bucket are not something I'm particularly proud of, but they are very revealing.

If I'm honest, I need to admit that my feelings are evidence that I am still very much embedded within a culture that equates status with expensive stuff. I cannot remove myself from my culture completely. Not all cultures are like ours in this respect. Some indigenous cultures equate status with wisdom or generosity, and there is little difference in how many material possessions members of the community have, no matter their status. Hoarding possessions by an individual is socially unacceptable. How different that is from our culture, where we judge others by their bank accounts, or at least what we perceive their bank accounts to be. To one degree or another, we all experience pressure to keep up appearances that are deemed appropriate to our social standing. Even in the midst of the economic collapse of recent years, many people still felt compelled to keep up the illusion of prosperity, even as they struggled to pay the bills. This phenomenon speaks volumes about our collective priorities. Tragically, dysfunctional American concepts of status are spreading. The *nouveau riche* class in emerging industrialized countries (especially China) is increasingly enamored with conspicuous consumption, and the growing middle class follows their lead.

The ongoing task of keeping up appearances is not only hazardous to our financial security; it's also hazardous to our collective ecological security. And we know it. We all know intellectually that endlessly increasing consumption is unsustainable for the Earth, but our behavior betrays a deeper psychology. The bottom line is that what others think of us matters. We want to be valued and respected. We want to be held in high regard by those around us. We want people, even strangers, to judge us favorably. These desires are as old as humanity itself and form the bedrock on which all the cultural pressures pile up. The work before us is not to try to change the bedrock (an impossible task) but rather to change the culture. This will be difficult, perhaps, but not impossible.

Practices

Neighborhood Walk Who are the proverbial "Joneses" where you live? What about them qualifies them for that nickname? Take a walk around your neighborhood. As objectively as you can (realizing that perfect objectivity is impossible), mentally note what constitutes status. Is it the biggest house? A certain type of car? Perhaps it's something more subtle, like the regular comings and goings of a decorator. Maybe in your area, status concepts are even a little eco-oriented, such as having solar panels on the roof. If you live in a city, how is status expressed for apartment dwellers? Is it the realtor's mantra of "location, location, location" or is it something else? How might status be expressed differently in a blue collar neighborhood than a white collar one? Does the state of the economy influence expressions of status? Think about what people might be trying to express through their outward symbols of status.

Childhood Walk This is a variation on the exercise above, so read through that one first. Find a quiet place where you will be undisturbed, and take an imagined mental walk down the streets of your childhood neighborhood. Visualize each house or apartment building, along with the cars, gardens, and people. Who had the fanciest house? Were all the houses similar? Who were the Joneses of your childhood? Recall your perceptions from child-hood. How did you perceive the people who lived around you? As a child, were you the top dog or the underdog? Did your family's economic status have an impact on how you were perceived? Was the neighborhood mixed in terms of income, or more homogenous? Take some time and journal about your memories.

Inner and Outer Life Clear your altar of any items used previously. On one side, place three or four items that symbolize your outer life and how the world perceives you. These items may symbolize your work, your socioeconomic status, your home, or any aspect of your identity that is open to the public eye. On the other side, place three or four items that symbolize your inner life. These items should symbolize aspects of you that are more personal and private. These may be religious or spiritual symbols, or items that represent any part of your life that the world does not see. Leave the items separated on the altar for a few days. Spend some time observing your creation and musing on its meaning. Next, rearrange the altar and remove any items that do not represent what you consider to be the real you. What's left? Is it a mix, or are the items now only from one side? Leave the new arrangement in place for a few days and observe what you've created. Rearrange it, adding or removing items intuitively.

Large Group—What's Your Bucket? Gather the group, and sit in a large circle. Group members can voluntarily share their personal "bucket" stories like mine, above. Have members share stories of when they were compared to others regarding material status or possessions in an uncomfortable or unfavorable way. Objective reality counts less here than how they felt about those experiences. The stories can be either from members' present-day lives or from a time in their past, even childhood. Recognize that stories may be quite personal. Be respectful of each person's unique experiences. Afterward, go around the circle and offer each person some encouraging words about their worth in non-economic terms, such as their friendliness, compassion, or creativity.

For Reflection

∾ Scriptures of many religious traditions contain parables, stories, or proverbs about the dangers of judging by outward appearances alone. What does your faith say on the subject?

∾ Have you ever been in the home of someone who was very status conscious and wealthy enough to fully express it? What was your emotional response to the experience? Were you at all envious? Be honest.

∾ If you have children, how do concepts of status impact their world? Do they feel pressure to keep up with the junior Joneses? How?

∾ How does our present culture reinforce concepts of status based on material possessions? What might status look like in a culture that truly valued ecological sustainability?

FIVE

Cogs in the Machine

Part of coming face to face with reality is realizing how much of our collective situation is truly out of our individual control. We live embedded within national and global systems over which we have absolutely no power. For example, we are citizens of a country whose government may do things—wage war, impose taxes, pass laws—with which we disagree. We may protest, or work to elect people whose actions may better reflect our own opinions, but there is a limit to our influence, individually or as a group. Even if we dedicate our lives to a particular cause, like ending logging in sensitive old growth forests, there are a thousand other equally worthy causes that won't receive our attention. Such is life. Looking past the big stuff like wars and taxes, we need to realize that every aspect of our lives—the food we eat, the cars we drive, the places we work, even the toilets we flush—has an impact on the environment, and precious little is totally within our control.

We live within systems bigger than ourselves. Realizing this can be disheartening and result in apathy. Environmentalist David Suzuki points out that too many negative headlines about the environment can result in a mentality where people simply disengage from the debate altogether, believing that it is entirely beyond our control and influence. This is an understandable response, although perhaps an overreaction. However, despite the risk of disengagement on the part of some, the first step toward recovering from our collective cultural addiction to the status quo is the recognition that we are powerless in the face of it. Chellis Glendinning calls this our techno-addiction, and calls us to face up to our powerlessness over it as a first step toward our cultural recovery.

Consider the following: Once upon a time, "Mr. Green" wanted to live an eco-friendly lifestyle. He worked for Giant Megacorp Industries and wasn't very happy about it, but he had children to support and jobs are hard to come by, so off to work he went. He recycled all he could at home and even struggled to save his money to put solar panels on his house. But he still worked for GMI because jobs are hard to come by, and he couldn't afford to quit. One day, GMI sent Mr. Green across the country on a big jet plane to an important convention where they served him factory-farmed food for his dinner. Every day, he handed out free goodies made of plastic to potential clients. He stayed at a Big Fancy Hotel where they changed his sheets and towels even when he told them not to do it. Mr. Green went home after the convention feeling guilty. He so wanted to help GMI become more eco-friendly, but his boss, Mr. Bigshot, didn't care. The boss got tired of hearing Mr. Green talk about eco-this and eco-that, and reminded him that jobs are hard to come by.

Sound familiar? There are thousands of Mr. and Ms. Greens out there today, doing the best they can in the real circumstances of their lives. We can accomplish a lot through individual choices, but we need to be aware of systems that are beyond our control. To change them, we may need to change laws, but more importantly we need to change the culture as a whole.

Decades ago, heavy smoking was commonplace. Nearly everyone smoked all the time. It was considered sophisticated and sexy. Today, non-smoking public spaces are the norm, and smoking carries with it a social stigma and is in decline in the United States and Europe. Why the change? Science proved how unhealthy it was to smoke, and laws were slowly changed to reflect that fact. More important was the change that took place in the culture. Smoking is no longer the mark of glamor or status it once was. Attitudes shifted. Most who do smoke want to quit, and the vast majority of people support keeping public spaces smoke-free.

To change the Earth-destroying systems that are beyond our control, we need to experience a soul-deep cultural attitude shift and rediscover the sacredness of the Earth. We have the scientific understanding, and the laws are a work-in-progress. The attitude shift is what is most urgently needed. Planet-destroying, do-what-I-want attitudes need to give way to Earth-restoring behavior the same way that smoke-filled offices gave way to cleaner indoor air. Facing up to the way things really are is a critical first step toward making the deep changes our society so desperately needs.

Practices

The Roller Coaster Find a comfortable, quiet place where you will be undisturbed. Imagine that you are getting onto a roller-coaster. Use memories to help you if you can. As you visualize, try to engage your whole body. Feel the wind in your hair, and that stomach-in-your-throat sensation from the ride. You sit, and the bar comes down. You're strapped in. The coaster starts to move, and you realize there's no turning back. You're on the ride now, no matter what. The operation of the coaster is in the control of others. Imagine yourself on the slow, jerky climb, the stomach-churning downward rush, and the twists and turns. Now, imagine that instead of stopping, the ride keeps on going, over and over. You feel queasy, but people around you seem to be having fun. You yell, but the people in the control booth can't hear you. You are strapped in. You can't get off. You're stuck unless something changes. Slowly, one by one, others start to feel sick like you do, and together you begin to shout to the people in the booth. How long before they hear? Ride the coaster a while in your mind, and think about all that is out of your control. The coaster is the culture. Are we shouting yet?

Note: If you are working through the book alone, you may find that you need to do one of the following to help you with this visualization: read it through several times until you can recall it for the visualization, have a friend read it to you, or record yourself reading it with appropriate pauses.

Ritual of Release Obtain a fireproof bowl and at least a dozen slips of paper. Place the bowl on your altar, and over the course of a week or so, write down some of the Earth-threatening things that are out of your control. For example, you might write "illegal logging in the rainforest" or "overfishing the world's oceans." Spend some time reading about the environment and you'll have no trouble coming up with things to write. As the bowl fills over the course of the week, spend a few minutes each day just being at your altar. Sit with it, and contemplate all that it implies. After a week, take the bowl outside and carefully burn the papers, symbolically releasing what you cannot control. Add the ashes to your garden.

Be a Little Subversive There may be a lot that we cannot control, but we can challenge the prevailing notions of society. If you are not the type to confront people openly about ecological issues, or if you're simply shy, a little subversion might just be the thing. You might take your old environmentally oriented magazines and leave them in waiting rooms instead of sending them straight to the recycling bin (cut off the address labels first). Or, you could get some small brochures from a voluntary simplicity or environmental group and leave one behind in every public restroom you use. You could be really sneaky and write on sticky notes things like "Do you really need to buy more stuff?" or "Americans are 5 percent of the world's population, but use 30 percent of the world's resources. Think about it." Then, stick these on mirrors in store dressing rooms or restrooms. These kinds of actions challenge the "business as usual" mindset and provide an antidote to our feelings of helplessness in the face of the powers-that-be. And—who knows?—you may inspire more change than you realize. Do the roller-coaster meditation before undertaking this practice. Action is needed, but we also need to face what we can't control.

Large Group—Ritual of Release For large groups, adapt the "Ritual of Release" altar work suggested above. Decorate your altar with symbols of modern life that are beyond the control of the individual. You can plan this in detail ahead of time, or simply have people add items that they have on their person (such as a cell phone to represent technology or a coin to represent monetary or tax policies), or items that you can find in your group's meeting space. Then, have everyone spend a few minutes thinking of areas of their lives that resemble the story of Mr. Green. Ask each group member to write down one example, and add it to a large bowl on the altar. Spend some time sharing as a group, then take the bowl outside and burn the papers. You could also combine this with a campfire or bonfire and burn the papers there. After that, simply sit in silence for a while. This is important. Don't rush things. After some time has passed, brainstorm ways that group members can support each other in challenging dominant attitudes. It's hard to be the voice crying in the wilderness. How can we lighten each other's burdens?

For Reflection

∾ In your personal life, have you ever felt swept up by circumstances beyond your control? Does this experience have anything in common with the experience of living in contemporary culture?

∾ Have you ever consciously done something harmful to the Earth simply because to do so was the path of least resistance? Did you feel guilty afterwards?

∾ List several charitable organizations that you support. What can you do to help their work? What factors are out of your control?

∾ We are all citizens of something, whether or not we approve of what governments do in our name. What is it about the system of government under which you live (national, local, or whatever) that makes it difficult to bring about deep cultural change?

SIX

Industrial Civilization and Everyone Else

On a bookshelf in my living room sits a bright and colorful book, full of interesting photos of children from around the world. The authors chronicled the small details of each child's life, such as a favorite toy or food. Although it's meant for children, it's the sort of book that you can open to any page and find something that catches your eye and holds your interest, no matter your age. The stories of the children's daily lives are fascinating, and very personal.

One photo of a little boy from Tanzania still draws me in every time I look at it. He isn't one of the children profiled in depth. His photo adorns only one page, along with photos of many other children from Africa. His name is Nicodemu, and he was eight years old in the early 1990s when the picture was taken. In the photo, he is half-smiling and looking off into the distance, away from the camera. He is wearing what looks to be a dirty cast-off rag that has been draped and knotted into a robe of sorts. He has sandals on his feet, but they don't fit very well. He holds two long sticks, perhaps used for herding or as walking sticks. The photo offers no information about the boy. Perhaps he was part of a loving family and had his most basic needs met, despite his appearance. I hope this is the case. He is by far the poorest-looking child on the page, and my heart breaks every time I lay eyes on his picture. More than once, his image has brought me to tears. When I see him, I want to give him a hug and a good meal.

Of course, I know he is only one child of millions, but statistical knowledge of the "millions" doesn't touch us like the image and story of one child. We are hard wired by evolution to respond to individual people, not statistics. Nicodemu is a young adult by now, if he is still alive at all. I'll never know what happened to him, but I expect that my thoughts and prayers will turn to him from time to time for the rest of my life. He has become a powerful symbol for me of the "rest of the world," which remains mostly out of sight for us in the wealthy West.

If the whole world lived a middle-class American lifestyle, it would take more than four Earths to provide the resources. This lifestyle can only be maintained if others around the world do not share it, and instead live in dire poverty. Resources are extracted, exploited, and unequally shared. We can argue till the cows come home about the reasons why, but this is the situation. Americans have a lot compared to Nicodemu, even those who live on a tight budget. We have way more than anything resembling our fair share, while others have so little. In fact, one of the biggest problems facing us globally is that the developing world aspires to a middle-class American standard of living, and those of us who have that keep raising the bar for ourselves. Author Peter Seidel reminds us, "The citizens of wealthy nations demand that their leaders continue to raise their standard of living—and they must do so simply to avoid unemployment and please business." And we know it, even if we don't like to admit it. So the disparities become ever greater.

None of this is the fault of us as individuals. We no more could control the circumstances and locations of our births than Nicodemu could control his. We were lucky. And although we cannot be blamed for the circumstances that led us to where we are today, we do have a responsibility to live with as much integrity and mindfulness as possible in our personal lifestyle choices. We need to say "enough" to our leaders and to the unrealistic notion that our standard of living should constantly rise. We need to say "enough" in our individual lifestyle choices. We owe Nicodemu and the millions like him nothing less.

Practices

Mindful Fast If you have never experienced fasting, consider doing so for a day or even just a single meal. Several charitable organizations sponsor fast days on college campuses, and students donate the money they would have spent on food to hunger relief projects. Religious congregations also participate in these events. However, it's not necessary to participate in a group event to have a meaningful experience. If you are medically able to do so, set aside a day to fast—preferably one in which you don't have a lot of outside obligations. A quiet, solitary retreat day is ideal. Spend some time in contemplation, meditation, or prayer. When you break your fast, do so gently and slowly with simple foods. A huge feast after a fasting day is a recipe for indigestion. As you fast, note the sensations of your body. Do they stay the same throughout the day, or do they change? Reflect on the feeling of emptiness—what meaning does it hold for you? Spend some time contemplating the haves and have-nots in our world. Does the experience of the fast influence your thinking? How?

Altar of the Empty Bowl Find a photo of a child from a poor country. Place it on your altar for several days, along with an empty bowl. Spend some time at the altar, considering what this child's daily life might be like. Don't over-romanticize the child. Acknowledge aspects of the child's life that may be positive, but don't gloss over the tough stuff either. Write your thoughts in your journal. After working with the altar like this, you may decide to sponsor a child or contribute to global anti-poverty efforts through a charitable organization. If you do, be cautious and investigate the organization that will receive your donation. Watchdog groups such as the American Institute of Philanthropy or Charity Navigator offer ratings for various relief organizations to ensure that donated money gets to the people who need it most.

Brainstorming Lifestyle Changes In your journal, or on a large blank piece of paper, brainstorm ideas about how you can make lifestyle changes that better reflect your values. Don't censor yourself. Write down anything that comes to mind, no matter how wild and impossible it may seem. Brainstorm for at least ten minutes. Now, set aside your list for a day or so. When you come back to it, ask yourself: What ideas resonate most strongly with you? What changes can you make? Make them.

Large Group—Host a Hunger Banquet The global relief organization Oxfam has developed a unique way for people to learn about global food resource distribution. Participants in Oxfam America's *Fast for a World Harvest* Hunger Banquet arrive at the banquet site and are randomly given designations based on income. The designations reflect real-world hunger distribution. People assigned to a rich table are fed a complete meal with food to spare. People in the middle receive a simple meal of beans and rice. The majority of people end up seated at poor tables, where they are given a small portion of rice alone. The dinner is a powerful catalyst for discussing issues of wealth distribution. Search online for menus, scripts for dinner announcements, and help in planning the event. You can also design your own banquet. This event is commonly used as a fundraiser for hunger relief organizations, but this is of course optional.

For Reflection

∽ Why do we respond to stories and photos of individuals who experience suffering, while ignoring suffering on a large scale?

∽ Why do well-intentioned solutions from rich countries sometimes backfire in poor countries and end up making poverty problems even worse?

∽ If Nicodemu were standing in front of you, how would you explain to him why the world is the way it is?

∽ Does a person like Nicodemu occupy a place in your heart? Perhaps a particular photo has stuck with you over the years, or you sponsored a child at some point. Maybe you encountered someone from a developing country while traveling. How has this person affected you? What do you remember about your encounter?

The Path of Un-Learning

The path of un-learning naturally, but not inevitably, follows the path of awakening. When confronted by uncomfortable realities, many of us retreat into denial rather than face the task of digging deeper into figuring out what caused those realities in the first place. This is especially true when digging deeper threatens the assumptions on which our lifestyle is based. Fortunately, this is not the only response. Every day around the world, people of all backgrounds are challenging the unhealthy and unsustainable physical systems and mental paradigms that fuel contemporary industrial society. The chapters in part two help to deconstruct some of the underlying assumptions and paradigms that sustain the business-as-usual mindset. They will help you dig a little deeper into why our culture is the way it is and serve as a catalyst for developing own ideas as well.

As with all the practices in this book, you may find that some resonate with you more than others. Don't feel obligated to methodically work through every one. Pick and choose according to your own personality and preferences. Discussing the questions at the end of the chapter with others is helpful, whether or not you are working with an established group, since the material of part two relates to aspects of our culture that are slightly below the surface. Excavating cultural paradigms and unspoken assumptions is easier when others can function as a sounding board for you. Of course, your insights will enlighten others as well. May your path be a rewarding one.

SEVEN

The Problems of Progress

To one degree or another, we are all enamored with the technological accomplishments of the modern world. Centenarians living today would have been born during the waning days of the horse and buggy. They grew up in a world where childhood diseases routinely took the lives of friends and family. They would have received their news from letters or newspapers alone. Throughout their lifetime, they have seen tremendous changes in communication technology, travel, medicine, and (unfortunately) the technology of warfare. The past century has been a dizzying ride, with constant change leading to unprecedented prosperity for those of us lucky enough to live in industrialized countries. Ask your elders about the changes they have seen. Progress is an amazing thing. Who knows what marvels the future will bring?

We love the notion that technology is the pinnacle of human accomplishment, and that humans are the most important living beings on earth. However, we don't like to look at the dark side of our technological achievements, or face up to the unintended consequences of all this progress. Bill McKibben writes in *Eaarth* that we are really living on a new planet (hence the new name in the title of his book)—a planet entirely different from the one on which we were born and the one on which civilization emerged. Industrial civilization has unwittingly altered the very support systems upon which we all depend—namely a stable, predictable, self-regulating biosphere—and the task before us is to learn how to live in this new, less friendly physical world. So much for progress!

Some years ago, I visited Ironbridge, England. It bills itself as the birthplace of the Industrial Revolution and is a UNESCO World Heritage Site. On the site there is an actual cast iron bridge, the first of its kind, built in 1779, as well as a museum displaying period technology. Surrounded by giant, antique iron works, I could not help but be overcome with a sense of sadness and foreboding. The behemoth rusting relics seemed to have an almost religious feel to them, as though the place was a kind of temple to the gods of industrialization.

When the iron works was built, the Earth was viewed by many people, but not all, as an inanimate resource without end, which existed for us to exploit as we saw fit. The dominant powers of the day were Christian and held biblically based ideas, especially since they could easily find passages in the Bible that supported an expansionist worldview. According to Genesis, we were placed here by the Creator to subdue the Earth. And subdue it we have. The ongoing legacy of that cast iron bridge is complicated and mixed. Its legacy is not only moon landings, heart transplants, and the Internet but also mountaintop removal mining, oceanic dead zones, an unpredictable climate, and depleted uranium. So far, we haven't figured out how to have the former without the latter. Renowned ecological philosopher Thomas Berry put it this way, "We have created a technosphere incompatible with the biosphere."

The path of un-learning is a path of letting go. We must let go of those things that no longer serve our highest good or that of the Earth, which are really one and the same. One of the most critical concepts to abandon is the notion of unproblematic progress. We must ask some hard questions, and not turn away from unpleasant answers. We must approach new technologies with a "do no harm" ethic and consciously examine the role of technology in our own lives. In this respect, I love the Amish. They are one group that never quite bought into the propaganda of industrialized progress. Ironically, many of them have integrated some modern products into their lives. They have cell phones, solar panels, and battery-powered devices. Contrary to popular belief, they all do not eschew technology completely. Rather, they are very selective. They choose only technologies that fit with their ethic of simplicity and their religious faith, and use their chosen items very carefully. An Amish friend of mine keeps his cell phone out in his shed and uses it only as necessary to run his farm. No family meals are interrupted by its annoying intrusion. The Amish are very conscious of technology and its impact—for good and ill—on their lives. We all must adopt a similar kind of consciousness, for from it flows a more balanced view of the fruits of industrialization. We also need to realize how technology is a part of our lives regardless of whether or not we can afford, or even want, the latest gadgets. We swim in a sea of microchips, from those that store our bank account and tax records to those that run the digital x-ray machine used to diagnose our child's broken arm. From 3-D movies to those automated phone calls that interrupt our dinner, technology is everywhere.

Progress comes with a price. Perhaps it is worth the cost, perhaps not. But here and now on our spiritual journey, we must embrace the questions about it—even if we don't have the answers worked out completely. This is the essence of living an awakened, examined life.

Practices

Give and Take The mindset that drove the Industrial Revolution from its beginning is alive and well today: aggressive self-centeredness, coupled with blindness to the consequences of endless growth. In essence, it is an attitude of take-take-take without any give. Long-term outcomes are denied, externalized, or simply not considered.

If you've ever gone to the beach, chances are that you've taken a few shells or interesting rocks home with you. If you live in an area where fall is a spectacular riot of changing color, you've probably picked up a few pretty leaves over the years. Most likely, you've done this without thinking. You have taken without giving back. We all have.

For this practice, choose one aspect of your life where you take from the Earth's bounty. Your food, perhaps. Or your electricity, which might come from coal. Or maybe you simply like to collect pretty rocks from the beach. Big or small, the idea is the same. Make a pact with yourself. Write it down if you like, and post it somewhere prominent to serve as a reminder. From now on, for your chosen area, each take will require a give. For example, if you are a beach pebble collector, you could also spend some time picking up litter on that same beach. If you chose food, you could volunteer at a soup kitchen, or organize some friends to purchase fair trade coffee as a group. The specific action is less important than cultivating the mindset that taking necessitates giving.

Technology Fast Here's your chance to think Amish. Choose one device your grandma didn't grow up with and turn it off for a week. This could be your TV, radio, computer, GPS system, or any other piece of technology that occupies a significant place in your life. On Sunday, ceremonially turn it off. Throughout the week, mentally reflect on, or even better, journal about the experience of living without your item. At the end of the week, decide whether or not to continue the fast. Recognize that there is no judgment implied here. Choosing to live without your device is not somehow more virtuous than turning it back on again. The point is to recognize that the choice is a conscious one, and to choose mindfully.

Stream of Consciousness Write continuously for at least ten minutes. Allow your thoughts to flow where they will. Try one or more of the following as your starter sentence, or make up one of your own. If you find you've exhausted the possibilities of one starter sentence before the ten minutes are up, pick another and keep on writing.

- If I had been alive three hundred years ago, my life . . .

- I like modern life, but . . .

- The Earth provides . . .

- If I had a time machine, and could go anywhere with it, I would . . .

Large Group—Elder Wisdom Invite several people who are more than eighty years old to share their life experiences with the group. Ask them: What has changed since you were children? What things are better now? What was better then? What do you see as the most significant area of human progress? What problems do you see for the future? What sort of world would you wish for future generations?

For Reflection

∾ What are some of the negative aspects of technology? How can we mitigate their effects?

∾ Provide one or two examples of technology that is superfluous or wasteful. What can or should we do about this waste?

∾ What criteria should we use to decide how much technology to allow into our lives? How can we approach technological progress in a mindful way?

∾ What must you personally unlearn in order to approach technology sustainably?

EIGHT

Images of Earth

One of the most famous images of all time is the photo of the Earth taken by the Apollo astronauts. Hanging in the black void of space, the Earth looks fragile, precious. All human history has taken place on the delicate blue jewel suspended in nothingness. This realization strikes a chord in our collective consciousness and has been especially influential on the modern environmental movement.

While this view of Earth from a distance is a powerful image, it doesn't inform the dominant paradigm of how we as a species think of our home planet. Instead, it is like a piece of art hanging in our mental gallery and mostly ignored. The dominant worldview is of Earth as an economic resource, divided by boundaries and borders. Many have a more romanticized understanding of Earth as provider, or even as mother, but the underlying concept is not that different. We may borrow the language of many indigenous cultures, who also conceptualize Earth as mother, but our actions speak of a different understanding —and they speak louder than our words. If we treated our human mothers the way we treat Mother Earth, we would be arrested for assault.

Even mainstream environmentalists have embraced the image of Earth as resource/provider. They may argue that we must protect a certain habitat because someday we might find a cure for cancer there. Or that we should develop eco-tourism to help the local economy. While there isn't anything inherently wrong about curing cancer or providing a livelihood for people who would otherwise be destitute, it reflects an underlying view that Earth's value comes only from its economic potential.

A more nuanced look at this paradigm reveals an even deeper concern. Conceptualizing the Earth in this way places Earth in the category of the Other—something outside ourselves that exists *for us*. It is separate from us, and thus can be exploited for our purposes. Susan Griffin, in her revolutionary work *Woman and Nature*, puts it this way: "All nature, it is said, has been designed to benefit man. That coal has been placed closer to the surface for his use. That animals run on four feet because it makes them better beasts of burden. That teeth were created for chewing, and that women 'exist only for the propagation of the race.'"

Stretching the idea, but only just a little, we not only see Earth as provider, but as limitless. All industrialized cultures, Americans in particular, are uncomfortable with limits. We like to see ourselves as having limitless potential, able to achieve anything. It's a nice fantasy, but an unhealthy one. Growth without limit is cancer. Everything has limits, and recognizing them is not only desirable but necessary at this point in human history. Back in the 1970s, the idea of consciously choosing to limit economic growth for the sake of preserving the environment was briefly considered. Those who recall that era may remember President Carter installing solar panels on the White House roof and telling Americans to conserve energy, while setting an example by putting on sweaters and turning down the thermostat. Needless to say, those ideas never caught on, and America subsequently embraced the idea of endless economic growth and prosperity embodied by Ronald Reagan.

In order to abandon the dominant paradigm of Earth as unlimited resource or endless provider, we need to find an image that can function in its place to inform our thinking and action. Certainly the visuals of Earth from space are helpful, but alone they are not enough. In a very literal sense, we are the Earth. Our bodies are made of the stuff of the Earth. The atoms and molecules that make up every part of us have been circulating around the biosphere since life began. The Earth is us and we are the Earth. What we do to the Earth, we ultimately do to ourselves. By letting go of the Earth as Other paradigm, we make space for the possibility of Earth as Self. By un-learning the mindset of the Earth as an endless provider, we begin to form a healthy sense of our own boundaries and limits, and learn to function within them. This mindset has been embraced by many indigenous cultures the world over for millennia. Rediscovering it may be the key to our survival.

Practices

Melting into the Earth On a warm day, go outdoors to a quiet place where you can be undisturbed for fifteen to twenty minutes. Lay down directly on the Earth, flat on your back or on your stomach. Spread your arms wide. Breathe slowly and deeply, and spend a minute or two just relaxing. When you feel relaxed, imagine yourself as water soaking into the Earth. There is no separation between you and the ground beneath you. The cells of your body flow into and between the cells of the soil, merging into oneness. Allow yourself to experience this completely. After fifteen to twenty minutes, slowly come back to normal awareness.

Compost Blessing If you don't already compost, I urge you to give it a try. Composting is a technique used by gardeners and farmers to naturally enrich the soil by adding decomposed plant matter such as leaves, grass clippings, and other waste. Small-scale composting of your kitchen scraps into a vegetable garden is easy, and the ultimate in recycling.

If you do compost, try the following: Next time you bring the compost out to the bin, bless it. Say a simple phrase, like "Blessings on your journey around the cycle of life," or offer a prayer of your own choosing. Consciously imagine the compost breaking down into rich soil, and then nourishing next year's tomatoes. Imagine yourself eating those same tomatoes, realizing that the compost, the tomatoes, and you are all part of a greater whole. Because you are.

Earth as Mother Write for at least a half hour on the concept of Earth as mother. Use any of the prompts below as a starting point for your explorations.

∾ Consider yourself as a child of the Earth. What sort of child are you? Where are you in your development? What is your personal relationship to Earth, your mother?

∾ Consider the same concept of being a child of the Earth, but this time, broaden the focus. Answer the questions above with all of humanity as the child.

∾ If the Earth is our mother, what sort of mother is she? What stage of motherhood works for the image nowadays? Is she a young mother? Elderly? Pregnant?

The mother-child relationship can also have a shadow side, dysfunctional and unhealthy. Is there a shadow side to the human-Earth relationship? What is it?

Large Group—Culture Quest Gather books or articles of indigenous creation myths from many cultures. Ideally, these should represent a diversity of locations as well as cultures. Break into smaller groups of three to four, and have each group read a myth. Discuss in the small groups how the Earth is envisioned in the myth, and how this differs, or doesn't, from the way we envision the Earth today. Consider the role of the human in each story. After a time in small groups, come together again as a larger group and share a brief summary of each myth, as well as the thoughts and insights of group members. Spend some time discussing the images of Earth in the larger group. Did one particular story resonate with your group? Why or why not?

For Reflection

∽ How do indigenous concepts of the Earth as mother compare and contrast to modern or Western understandings of this idea ?

∽ How does classifying something as Other affect how we think about it?

∽ The mainstream environmental movement often frames its arguments based on the idea of preserving the Earth as a resource for human use (for example, the possibility of discovering new medicines in the endangered rainforest). Do you find this approach helpful or problematic? Why?

∽ Is it possible to assign economic value to all the Earth provides us? Would this be helpful or harmful?

NINE

The Right to Life

Autumn came to the forest. Gradually, the colors changed. Day by day, light and shadow shifted as the Earth tilted away from the sun. Acorns fell. Animals prepared for winter, as always. Some stored food. Some prepared to hibernate. Others left for warmer places. Still others died, leaving behind the next generation, safely ensconced in their eggs until the time of their emergence next spring. The river grew colder. The seasonal drama of life and death played itself out yet again, following the same script it had followed since the glaciers receded from the land millennia ago.

The human animal is the only creature we know of who consciously examines that script. Grabbing it from Nature's hands, we edit it. We alter the scenery, rewrite the dialogue, and do our level best to give ourselves the primary roles. The animals in the autumn wood live and die never having pondered the abstract concept of life itself. Only we do that. Full of bluster, we declare that we have a right to live. Not only that, but we have a right to live how, when, and where we choose. If we decide to bulldoze that forest to build a subdivision, we are entirely within our rights to do so. If someone

should ask about the rights of the forest creatures and their elaborate prepa-
rations for the coming cold, we don't have an answer. The question itself
borders on absurdity, and never crosses our minds.

Susan Griffin captures this traditional view perfectly in the following
passage from *Woman and Nature*. Describing a logger from the 1800s who
has discovered a new frontier, she writes,

> He is like a man in a dream who has discovered a treasure. He has come
> upon a forest untrod by human beings for hundreds of years. . . . In a
> trance, he makes figures. The numbers of the trees. Their size. Three
> to four million board feet for every forty acres, he whispers to himself.
> Centuries of growth. Centuries of rainfall. The very moisture of the air
> is golden. . . . By autumn, trees falling, moving upstream . . .

Nowadays, we might consider the fate of the forest if it contains creatures
we have designated as endangered, and therefore worthy of our attention
and protection. We might consider its value for recreational uses, or even
its value as a carbon sink to remove the greenhouse gases we pump into the
air. But to assign the forest existential rights is to elevate it, to raise it into
territory previously occupied only by ourselves. Thomas Berry is one of
only a few contemporary thinkers who have considered this possibility. In
The Great Work, he writes, "So too every being has rights to be recognized
and revered. Trees have tree rights, insects have insect rights, rivers have
river rights, mountains have mountain rights. So too with the entire range
of beings throughout the universe."

Taking the concept a step further, James Lovelock considers the Earth
itself as a living organism. In *Gaia: A New Look at Life on Earth*, he writes,
"From a Gaian viewpoint, all attempts to rationalize a subjugated biosphere

with man in charge are as doomed to failure as the similar concept of benevolent colonialism."

In the previous chapter, "Images of Earth" (page 45), we considered the idea of Earth as Self, rather than Other. Seeing the Earth this way is not an airy, "spirituality-lite" sort of idea. It is a truth in the most literal sense possible. It is also an ancient idea that resides deep within our collective psyche. Intuitively, we know it to be true, but for thousands of years Western culture has taught us otherwise. Letting go of this cultural programming demands that we acknowledge that the forest itself, considered as a collective, living whole, has a right to live out the patterns of its natural existence, to enact the script nature has written for it. It has earned this right by surviving, evolving unique adaptations, and creating a complex dynamic equilibrium that we humans are only beginning to comprehend.

This does not mean that the chipmunks, maple trees, and barred owls in the forest have more rights than humans. Rather, viewing the forest as an aspect of the living Earth and an extension of the self requires us to be cautious, taking no more than we need to live and approaching it with reverence and humility. Hindus use the greeting *Namaste*, loosely translated as "The holy in me bows to the holy in you." Looking at the natural world through spiritual eyes—seeing it as a reflection and extension of our ourselves, and ourselves as a reflection and extension of it—leads us to a Namaste moment with the nearby forest and the larger Earth community. We unlearn the cultural programming that elevates humanity over all else. We return to our natural state. We let go of the narrow idea that only humans can hold or confer existential rights, and realize that the right to simply exist encompasses the greater whole.

Practices

Namaste Take a mindful walk, as described in chapter one, "Beginning with Love" (page 5), but this time walk in a natural area such as a park or nature trail. As you walk, pause now and then, and have a Namaste moment with a tree, flower, bird, cloud, or whatever aspect of nature holds meaning for you. Realize that you and the object are both ultimately made of the same stuff—Earth. You are both made from carbon, oxygen, nitrogen, and more, all dancing together in infinite and beautiful combinations.

Giving Voice to the Forest If the forest described above could speak, what would it say? Would it see itself as a whole, or as the sum of infinite parts? Would it see humans as an aspect of itself? Use your imagination, and allow the forest to introduce itself to you. Spend at least a half hour on this exercise. If you wish, write your experiences in your journal afterwards.

Loving-kindness Prayer In the Buddhist tradition, there are many examples of loving-kindness or "metta" meditation or prayer. Usually, an idea (such as peace) is repeated and expanded upon. For example, one may pray, "May I be at peace. May my family be at peace. May my community be at peace." Continue to pray, using many variations of the single phrase. The idea is to broaden the vision to include the larger world within one's circle of concern. Use the phrases below to get you started, and tap into your own creativity as you pray. See how deep and wide your circle of concern, can become.

∼   May this land be healed and restored . . .

∼   Blessings to this tree . . .

∼   May all beings live abundantly . . .

Large Group—Re-Imagining the Earth as Primary Thomas Berry once said that the Earth is primary and the human is derivative. The root of our contemporary environmental problems is that we have stood this truth on its head and acted as if the opposite were true. For this group exercise, divide the large group into groups of four to five people. Have each small group imagine what sort of society would exist if we structured our legal system to reflect the Earth as primary and the human as derivative. What would such a society look like? How would our government, courts, and legal system be different? How would our educational system be different? How would we earn a living? Would our monetary systems be different? How?

Spend at least a half an hour in small groups, working out the answers to these and any other questions that come up in the course of discussion. Gather again as a large group, and share thoughts and ideas. Finally, reflect as a large group on what members needed to unlearn and let go of in order to imagine this society.

For Reflection

∾ What does it mean to have a right to live? Who has this right? Individual species or ecosystems? Human only or non-human?

∾ When the needs of human and non-human life conflict, should the human automatically prevail? How should we decide?

∾ Is there ever a time when we should give preference to the needs and rights of non-human life ahead of human life?

∾ What sort of attitudes must we unlearn if we are to consider the possibility of non-human life having existential rights?

TEN

Rethinking Genesis

Okay, I know what you're thinking. You left behind the whole Adam-Eve-snake-apple story a long time ago, so let's just skip this chapter and move on. Not so fast. While it's true that nowadays not everyone takes Genesis' tale of creation and subsequent fall literally, the significance of this story goes beyond our personal beliefs. It gave rise to cultural attitudes that remain with us today, after centuries of having that narrative at the center of our belief system. Its underlying view of the natural world is still part of our collective consciousness.

I've heard many interpretations of the fall narrative of Genesis 3. Some view it as an allegory for the transition from a hunter-gatherer lifestyle to an agricultural one. Others interpret it as a culturally symbolic tale of the demotion of some deities and the ascendance of others. Still others interpret it as showing the favor of a deity for the lifestyle of nomadic pastoralists over a lifestyle of sedentary farming. Perhaps all of these interpretations contain elements of the truth.

The mythic origins of the story are from the Fertile Crescent. This area, the birthplace of Western civilization, witnessed the invention of written language, the beginnings of the rule of law, and the invention of agriculture. The three major religions of the Book—Judaism, Christianity, and Islam—all trace their roots to this area via the Babylonian origins of parts of Genesis. It's not surprising that origin myths from this region influenced the cultures of the West for millennia.

We find the essence of the problem in Genesis 3:17, where God curses the Earth itself. The soil is literally cursed, and Adam must then struggle to extract a living from it. Instead of experiencing Earth as holy, which was (and is) the norm for indigenous cultures around the world, the cultural heirs of Genesis viewed the Earth as a vehicle for punishment, an enemy, a cursed thing, filthy and corrupt. Needless to say, the association of women with all things earthly did nothing to enhance their status. The whole Earth-as-enemy idea grew and morphed over time. By the late Middle Ages, the dominant worldview declared that to reject all earthly things—including bodily functions and desires—was the path to godliness. Gradually, as the medieval mindset gave way to earliest modernity, the overt story of Genesis faded somewhat, but the underlying paradigm remained. Total mastery of the Earth became a driving vision of the Enlightenment and subsequent Industrial Revolution. Suddenly we were in charge. We built cities and factories. We moved away from the farms, from the muck and mud of a life lived close to Nature. We invented technologies. We cured diseases. And today, we live our lives in shrink-wrapped sterility, disconnected from the natural world and its processes.

The Western cultural drive to control and dominate the natural world stems from the deep taproot of the Genesis narrative, and continues to this day. On our path of un-learning, we must look closely at the social milieu that surrounds us and let go of the cultural paradigm that declares the Earth to be cursed, corrupt, and in need of domination.

Practices

Back to the Source If it's been a while since you've read it, take some time and slowly read chapters one through three of Genesis. What is your reaction? How does your emotional response differ from how you would have responded earlier in your life? Has your attitude toward Genesis changed? If so, how? Write your thoughts in your journal.

Blessed, Not Cursed Find a quiet place outdoors for the following meditation. Consider all that is needed for life—air, water, food, shelter, energy, and so on. Consider all that makes life more than simply existence, such as beauty, inspiration, connection, and love. Now, either aloud or silently, recite a litany of how you are blessed by the Earth. Here are a couple phrases to get you started:

∾   I am blessed. The Earth provides oxygen for me to breathe.

∾   I am blessed. As I gaze at the sunset, I am in awe of the beauty around me.

Make your litany both personal and universal. See yourself as a part of the Earth, and contemplate what it means to be blessed.

Differing Views of God In both the Christian and Jewish scriptures, there are views of God that contrast with that found in Genesis 3. Various authors in these texts portray God as caring for the Earth and its creatures. Consider the following:

Look at the birds of the air; they neither sow nor reap nor gather into barns, and yet your heavenly Father feeds them. Are you not of more value than they? And can any of you by worrying add a single hour to your span of life? And why do you worry about clothing? Consider the lilies of the field, how they grow; they neither toil nor spin, yet I tell you, even Solomon in all his glory was not clothed like one of these.

—Matthew 6:26–30

In his hand are the depths of the earth;
    the heights of the mountains are his also.
The sea is his, for he made it,
    and the dry land, which his hands have formed.
O come, let us worship and bow down,
    let us kneel before the Lord, our Maker!
For he is our God,
    and we are the people of his pasture,
    and the sheep of his hand.

—Psalm 95:3–7

You make springs gush forth in the valleys;
    they flow between the hills,
Giving drink to every wild animal;
    the wild asses quench their thirst.
By the streams the birds of the air have their habitation;
    they sing among the branches.
From the lofty abode you water the mountains;
    the earth is satisfied with the fruit of your work.

—Psalm 104:10–13

How do these differ from the image of a God who would curse the Earth?

Large Group—Giving Voice to Genesis This exercise was inspired by Joanna Macy's vision of a "Council of all Beings," which was in turn inspired by Native American thought. Stage an impromptu improvisation of the story of Genesis 3. Assign various group members to play the parts of Adam, Eve, God, and the Serpent. But don't stop there. Assign someone to play the part of the Tree of Knowledge, the Tree of Life, the Earth itself, the rivers of Eden, and the other animals and plants.

Decide if you want the story to be played out as written or not. Perhaps your group prefers to let the story flow freely, without a predetermined outcome. Consider trying it several different ways. Allow people a few minutes to get comfortable with their characters, and then go for it. See how the story unfolds when more characters speak than the traditional few.

Afterward, reflect on the experience, and allow characters to add any insights that were not spoken during the improvisation.

For Reflection

~ For all its problems, might there still be some wisdom to be found in the story of the fall? What is it? Is it relevant to only individuals, or to the entire culture?

~ Should Genesis 3 be understood to have cultural significance but nothing more? Should we move on and leave it behind?

~ Historically speaking, how has the idea of the Earth as an enemy or an object for domination played itself out?

~ Can we as a culture let go of the image of Earth as our adversary and a thing to be conquered? What would that mean for our society?

ELEVEN

The Vending Machine God

One of the silver linings from the financial collapse of 2008 is the rethinking of the "gospel of health and wealth," widely preached in the 1990s. This ideology maintained that God wanted people to have the big house, car, boat, or whatever, and to enjoy a luxurious lifestyle. It was a modern-day twist on the old idea that wealth was a sign of God's favor—and that the poor deserve to be poor. Never mind that it stood the core teachings of the Jewish and Christian scriptures on their head.

If you've not yet read chapter four, "How Much Is Enough?" (page 19), take a moment and do so now. There, we confront contemporary concepts of status. To heal the Earth and live in this emerging new world, we must let go of these, but it doesn't end there. Underlying the surface concepts of material status are more profound psychological beliefs that declare material things to be a source of deep contentment and life satisfaction. Whether or not we bought into the overt health and wealth gospel, it is not easy to let go of the paradigm of seeking contentment from material possessions. Especially since the turn of the twentieth century, advertisers have aggressively worked to convince us that we can find happiness and life satisfaction if only we would purchase whatever they happen to be selling at the moment. Since the early 1960s, they have used psychology in increasingly subtle ways, playing on our deepest longings for acceptance, love, inner peace, and contentment. It is impossible for us not to have absorbed at least some of this message. For working class people especially, the idea that wealth is a sign of God's blessing is particularly cruel. The monopoly game that is our financial system makes it very difficult for someone living paycheck to paycheck to achieve any real financial stability and accumulate wealth. Fortunately, when we recognize the health and wealth gospel for what it is and bring it into our conscious minds, we can begin to let it go.

There are two aspects of faith in the Vending Machine God, and we must let go of both of them. The first is believing in an insert-prayers-get-stuff sort of God. This is the health and wealth deity of recent economic boom years, who fortunately has begun to fade from our collective consciousness. This vision of God, along with consumerism as a whole, has been challenged in recent years by various groups who take seriously the social justice message of the ancient Hebrew prophets. One such group is Alternatives for Simple Living, who overtly confront the excesses of holiday consumption through their publications. More recently, they have connected voluntary simplicity more directly with environmental causes.

The second aspect of faith in the Vending Machine God is more pervasive, and less obvious. It is more than a desire for basic financial security—it is the belief that deep satisfaction will come from the next purchase. In this understanding, the vending machine itself is the God. Imagine one of those machines filled with toys in a big glass container. At the top of the container is a three-pronged arm that can be used to try to pick up a toy and deposit it into the chute to the outside. Imagine yourself as a child. After popping in your coins, you have a limited time to grab the toy you want. Of course, it is probably on the bottom, and the grasping hooks don't work very well. Your frustration increases as you try and try to grab the toy. After popping in several rounds of coins, you finally manage to extract it. You take it home, only to find that it just wasn't as great as you thought it was. You think that another one was surely better, so you grab another handful of coins and back to the arcade you go.

Endless pursuit of the next possession, experience, or situation to the exclusion of cultivating contentment in simple pleasures and grounding ourselves in the natural world is the adult version of being the kid at the vending machine. We chase illusions, oblivious to the utterly beautiful Earth on which we live. But the Earth is calling to us. It says: Let go, unlearn, come home.

Practices

Bookshelf Rethink If you saw yourself in the description of the kid at the vending machine, perhaps it's time for a mindful look back before letting go. Sort through the various spiritual and self-help books you've accumulated over the years with an eye for what really resonates and what doesn't. Are there any health and wealth sorts of books in your collection? What do you recall about your life circumstances when you purchased or received them? Looking at them now, do they still have any value for you? Is there something you can glean from them, or do you wonder why you ever got them in the first place?

After considering each book, ask yourself if there are any in the collection that you could let go of. Can they be given to charity? Maybe there's one that's so awful you want to send it straight to the trash. That's okay. It's entirely your choice.

Simplicity, Simplicity Clear your altar of all decoration, and give it a good dusting. Look around your home at objects that might be suitable for placing on your altar. Choose one. Place it on the altar and simply sit and ponder it for a while. Consider the meaning that your object holds for you. What does it symbolize? Can you find several meanings to it? Leave it there for a week or so, and sit with it several times, pondering some more. See if other meanings come to light over time. After the week has passed, switch your object for another one and try the process again. Do not rush into switching objects, and do not purchase anything new for the exercise. Work only with what you have, and find or create meaning as you go.

Chart Your Journey This is a good exercise for those who are visual thinkers, or those who like to quantify things. Take a sheet of plain white paper, and draw a horizontal line near the bottom of the page. Now, draw a vertical line up from the center of the horizontal one. The whole drawing should look like an upside-down capital "T." On one end of the horizontal line, write the words spiritual confusion/frustration, or something similar. On the other side, write spiritual contentment/peace, or something similar.

Now, starting at the bottom, where the horizontal line meets the vertical one, write your birth year. At the top of the vertical line, write the present year. Then draw a graph representing your own spiritual journey, marking a meaning line from the bottom to the top. The vertical line in the center represents a neutral state and the right and left edges represent opposite extremes. You'll probably end up with a wavy or zigzag sort of line that roughly shows the broad sweep of your spiritual life.

Look at that broad sweep and consider your beliefs, practices, and life events. Ask yourself: Were there times when you were living like the kid at the machine full of toys? When were the times of greatest growth? You may find that times of confusion and frustration were actually times of growth. Reflect on the concepts of consumerism and materialism as you examine your graph. Consider whether there were times in your life when accumulating material things was very important to you. Perhaps you felt pressured by working with status-conscious people. Maybe you embraced consumerism wholeheartedly when you got your first job or bought your first home. How do these times in your life relate to the spiritual aspects of your life?

Large Group—Your Common Journey Have each member of your group do the Chart Your Journey practice, above. Then gather together to look for patterns and commonalities. You don't need to share the personal details of your experiences unless you want to. Look at how the graphs compare during the time of childhood. Ask one another if you experienced spiritual crises in adolescence or midlife. After a time of comparison, discuss any patterns you found and make guesses as to why. Try to consider consumerism and materialism in your discussions. Be gentle and supportive of one another as you share.

For Reflection

∿ How does the insert-prayer-get-stuff kind of God fit with the overall zeitgeist of the twentieth century? As the consumption patterns of the twentieth century prove to be unsustainable, how might this image of God shift in response?

∿ Have you ever heard the message of any health and wealth preachers or advocates first hand? What was your reaction?

~ Have you heard any spiritual teaching that struck you as psychologically manipulative? Did it utilize any health and wealth elements?

~ Can simplicity also be a kind of abundance? How?

TWELVE

Letting Go and Moving Forward

Change is not easy for most people. There is a certain comfort in familiarity, even if that familiarity is dysfunctional or unpleasant. Internal, heart-level change is perhaps the most difficult kind. Deconstructing comfortable ways of being in the world, rethinking identity, and letting go of those beliefs that no longer function for us are challenging work. And yet, that is exactly what needs to happen on a cultural level at this juncture in human history. As a culture, we need to deconstruct, rethink, let go. It's easier said than done. It's hard enough to struggle with transformation on an individual level, even before considering the larger scale.

Our task, "the Great Work of our time" as Roman Catholic priest and author Thomas Berry so aptly put it, is to transform our relationship to the Earth. To reclaim the Holy Ground. To re-sacralize, re-sanctify, rebuild, rei-magine everything. In terms of the hero's journey described in chapter one, "Beginning with Love" (page 3), we are at a liminal place. Shedding the old, we have yet to create the new. We are at the turning of the tide, the pause between breaths. There are no guarantees of success. There are no certainties that the larger culture will ever be truly transformed. And yet here we are. Having faced the way things are, we are no longer content to live with blinders on, mindlessly. The transformation of our personal way of being is under way. Regardless of what the culture does or does not do, we embrace our life's task, our own personal Great Work. And we let go.

We let go of the idea of an endless, unlimited Earth. We let go of blind faith in silver-bullet solutions. We struggle to let go of our addiction to stuff, to consumerism, to symbols of success and status. We wrestle with ourselves, letting go. We struggle. We let go of quiet desperation. We let go of "more is better." We take two steps forward and one step back. We let go of thinking of ourselves and our actions as disconnected from the larger whole. We let go of outdated ideas and images. We let go of spiritual concepts primarily born from justifications of our own desires. We let go, and then let go some more.

In the middle of all this letting go, it's easy to feel like you're in a free fall. Having let go of so much, you may feel unsure of what happens next. To be disconnected from the dominant cultural paradigm but not really grounded in anything new is unsettling, but you won't be here forever. The in-between place is a temporary but necessary stopover in the process of change. This is true of any kind of transformation, but especially for a spiritual one. Author David C. Korton has termed this process "the Great Turning," where we turn away from a paradigm of empire—where hostility and competitiveness reign—and move toward a new paradigm of Earth community, in which a cooperative, balanced way of being emerges. Letting go of the mindset of empire, we take a deep breath, clasp hands, and turn.

Practices

The Path So Far If you are reading this book straight through, spend some time reviewing parts one and two. If you're cycling through the book or dipping in here and there, spend some time looking back on the material you've covered so far. What chapters resonated most strongly with your life experience? What ideas did you find troubling? Most interesting? Do you have a favorite practice? Reflect on why it is your favorite, writing down your thoughts, if you wish.

Ritual of Release On small slips of paper, write down old attitudes, ways of thinking, and beliefs that no longer resonate with your spirit. You may choose to do this with an exclusively ecological theme, or you may also include thoughts that do not directly affect the Earth. These slips of paper symbolize what you are letting go of.

Place the papers in a fireproof bowl and take them outdoors. Carefully burn them in a place that is sheltered from the wind. Add the resulting ash to your garden or compost pile. Reflect on the process of letting go, and its impact on you personally.

Rocks and Apples Read through this visualization two or three times, and then sit comfortably in a place where you will be undisturbed for fifteen minutes or so. Relax, and slow your breathing. Close your eyes, and just continue breathing for a few moments. Now, imagine yourself walking a long, dusty road that continues off into the distance. In your arms are several heavy bags full of rocks. On your back, you wear a pack filled with more rocks. You have rocks in your pockets too. You can't seem to recall where the rocks came from or how you got them, but you were told a long time ago that they were important, and carrying rocks was just what everyone did. No one questioned why.

As you trudge along, you realize how heavy the rocks are. It dawns on you that there doesn't seem to be a good reason to keep carrying them, but you are nervous about setting them down. You decide to try letting go of a little at a time. You take one out of your pocket and leave it on the side of the road. Nothing happens, except that your pocket is not as heavy. You go a little further, and decide to try it with another. Again, nothing happens. You go a few more steps, and then dump the entire load from your pockets. It feels nice, so you decide to ditch the bags of rocks as well. Ahhh . . . lovely.

You walk more quickly and comfortably, and pass an apple tree on the side of the road. You realize that since your pockets aren't filled with rocks that you can fill them with apples instead. A little further along, you remember the pack on your back, and stop to dump out all the rocks. You keep walking, encountering all sorts of wonderful people as you go. The journey goes on, and you, unburdened from the heavy load, happily continue. After you complete the visualization, bring your awareness back to the present, and open your eyes slowly.

Now, try the visualization again, but this time make your own variations to the scenario. Who might you encounter on the way? What else might you carry? Allow your own creativity the freedom to make it especially meaningful to you.

Note: If you are working through the book alone, you may find that you need to do one of the following to help you with this visualization: read through it several times until you can recall it for the visualization, have a friend read it to you, or record yourself reading it with appropriate pauses.

Large Group—Letting Go You've reached the halfway point in your spiritual journey together. Perhaps your group has changed since you started. New members may have arrived, and a few may have left. Even if the group has not experienced this sort of change, some sort of internal change has occurred in the individual members. Maybe it's a new attitude, or a rethinking of old ideas. Maybe some members have consciously changed their lifestyle in some way. Now is your chance to mark that change and support each other.

Design a ceremony or service to reflect the theme of letting go of old concepts. Incorporate music, special readings, and visual elements such as your altar. Make sure to allow time for people to briefly speak on the theme of letting go. This can involve simply going around the circle and completing the phrases, "I've faced up to . . ." and "I've let go of . . ." Alternatively, you may decide to be more formal, and create an entire church service around the theme. Or you may choose something in-between. Make it special for your unique group and its members.

For Reflection

∾ What does the process of unlearning mean to you? How do you choose which ideas to let go of and which to keep?

∾ Have you ever let go of something and felt unburdened and empowered by doing so? When? How did the process of letting go change you?

∾ As you consider the whole idea of unlearning and letting go, are there some ideas or concepts that are worth holding on to? What is it about them that makes them special and worth keeping even as you let go of others?

~ What cultural ideas or attitudes have been the most difficult for you to unlearn? Is there anything in particular that causes a real struggle for you? What is it, and why do you think it is so?

III

The Path of Discovery

When we walk the path of discovery, we start to recall the wisdom found deep in our bones—that we are part of something greater than ourselves, that despite our technological advances we are not gods, and that we are not separate from the world around us. This path calls us into an intuitive understanding of who we are and of our place in the world. Even though the scientific insights mentioned here—such as deep time or the vastness of the universe—may be new to us, we feel a deep sense of coming home when we integrate these concepts into our spiritual lives. Much of what science tells us today has always been intuitively understood by traditional, indigenous cultures. But for us who carry the cultural baggage of a belief in humanity's inherent superiority, it can be unsettling. Even so, in the end what we discover is who we really are.

In part three of this book, we come to a turning point. After facing unpleasant realities and deconstructing our cultural paradigms, we may be more open to new ways of being. But before embarking on the path of creation, we must ground ourselves in a new way of thinking about ourselves and our world. The ideas in this section can be profoundly spiritual and deeply moving, regardless of our theology or religion. Allow them to soak into your spirit, and you will find yourself renewed.

THIRTEEN

Deep Time Journeys

Of all the ways to cultivate a healthy sense of perspective, contemplating deep time is one of the best. The term was coined by natural history writer John McPhee in the early 1980s to refer to the countless millennia of the universe's existence. It is difficult to fully grasp the billions of years that make up the history of the universe, or even the history of Earth. We simply aren't wired to think in such terms. Usually, an analogy works best. If, for example, the history of Earth was condensed down to a single year, humans would not arrive on the scene until 11:59 p.m. on December 31. Another analogy supposes that the length of a football field represents a timeline. With one end zone representing the formation of earth and the other representing the present, the time since the emergence of humanity would encompass only a few centimeters.

Our arrival on Earth was quite sudden when considered from the perspective of the Earth itself. It is as though Gaia blinked, and suddenly found all of us here! But blink again, and we will pass like smoke on the breeze. Life, and the Earth, will go on without us. This realization can have a profound impact on how we view ourselves as a species. Do we honestly believe that our contemporary lifestyle can continue for millions of years to come? Do we really think that *homo sapiens* will endure and thrive as ancient species, like sharks or some insects have? If we're honest, most of us will realize that this is unlikely. Our species will continue for centuries and maybe millennia. But it is highly doubtful that we will survive for a geologic epoch or more.

If we take that metaphor of condensing the Earth's life down to a year, and extend it into the future for another year, we might find ourselves remaining on the scene for two or three more minutes, then disappearing again while earth continues on without us. If we add another football field to our metaphorical one, we could be generous and allot ourselves an inch or so at the boundary between the two. Many other species will probably leave along with us, mostly those who have walked on the field in the last few yards, such as the blue whale, Siberian tiger, and mountain gorilla. Sadly, our actions as a species will have prompted this exodus. The truly enduring life forms, our single-celled siblings, will continue happily onto the second field without us.

Some people find this knowledge uncomfortable and disconcerting. After all, we humans like to think that we are the center of the universe, and the pinnacle of creation. When we are knocked off that exalted perch, it can be a bit shocking. After we pick ourselves up again and ponder the implications of our brief time on Earth, we may instead find that the knowledge of the deep past and future might actually be comforting. We realize that we are part of a story much greater than our own, the grand story of life itself. Ursula Goodenough, in *The Sacred Depths of Nature*, puts it this way:

> We are one of perhaps 30 million species on the planet today, and countless millions that have gone before. . . . We are called to acknowl-

edge our dependency on the web of life both for our subsistence and for countless aesthetic experiences: spring birdsong, swelling tree-buds, the dizzy smell of honeysuckle. We are called to acknowledge that which we are not: we cannot survive in a deep-sea vent, or fix nitrogen, or create a forest canopy, or soar 300 feet in the air and then catch a mouse in a spectacular nosedive.

This story is indeed so much bigger than our one species, and yet our story is inextricable from *the* story.

Looking through the lens of deep time, we can see humanity more clearly as a precious and rare spark of Earth's self-awareness. We embody the Earth no less than mountains and seas embody the Earth. We are *of* the Earth. For the brief moment of our existence, we literally *are* the Earth, suddenly and fleetingly self-aware. Perhaps we are the prototype of Earth's consciousness. Perhaps, far in the future, evolution will once again produce beings such as ourselves, though we can only hope they would be wiser and more grateful for the shining moment of their existence.

Water Visualization Our bodies are mostly made of water, which not only flows through our veins but permeates every cell of our bodies. This water was created when our planet formed, along with the rest of the evolving solar system, billions of years ago. It has circulated from clouds to streams, rivers, oceans, and back again. It has been taken up by plants and sipped by dinosaurs. It has whirled in hurricanes, flowed through underground caverns, and evaporated from ponds.

Find a comfortable place for meditation. Sit or lie down, then focus your attention on the water molecules within you. In your mind's eye, trace their journey back through the centuries. Consider that Jesus, Muhammad, and

Confucius drank a few of those same water molecules. Follow them back to the time of earliest humans. Imagine the now extinct hominid *Australopithecus* drinking the water with cupped hands,.

Keep journeying slowly backward in time, before humans, before mammals, before dinosaurs, back to the primordial seas alive with trilobites. It's the same water that now flows in you. Keep imagining, back to the earliest one-celled life, and even before life began. It's still the same water.

Now, move forward in time. Realize that the same water will continue its journey long after humans are gone. Consciously bless the water within you, along with all the life it will nurture for ages to come.

Practices

Deep Time Altar Clear your altar of items, then place upon it symbols of the Earth as it existed before humans. For example, stones can symbolize mountains or tectonic plates. A leaf, pinecone, or flower can symbolize the plant kingdom, which has flourished on Earth for hundreds of millions of years. A feather or figurine of an animal might represent animal life. A small bowl of water can stand for ancient seas. Be creative. When you've completed the altar, sit with it and ponder your place in this grand epoch of life.

A more ambitious variation of a deep time altar can be created over the course of a year. On January first, select an altar spot, and clear it off. Place on it a symbol of the earliest single-celled life—perhaps a piece of confetti from the night before. Over time, gradually add symbols of more complex life, such as multi-celled forms, plants, and invertebrates. To find out when to add symbols of the later life forms, do a little research on Earth's history or use the following approximate dates as a guideline:

- January 1: earliest life appears

- January 27: photosynthesis evolves

- June 15: first cells with a nucleus

- October 24: first multicellular organisms

- November 8: earliest land plants appear

- December 4: age of dinosaurs begins

- December 24: age of dinosaurs ends with asteroid impact

- December 31, 1:30 p.m.: earliest proto-humans

- December 31, 11 p.m.: earliest modern humans

- December 31, a few seconds before midnight: earliest human civilizations, recorded history begins

Allow your altar to fill up throughout the year. Finally, on the following New Year's Eve, right before midnight, add your symbol for human civilization.

Reflect on the experience of creating your altar throughout the year. Bear in mind that for much of the year, your pieces of confetti will have the altar to themselves, and that most additions will occur late in the year. This in itself can be enlightening. A slowly growing deep time altar can be a wonderful experience.

Deep Time Meditation Visit a museum of geology or natural history, and approach the exhibits with a contemplative mindset. Engage your spirit as well as your brain. Wander the exhibits of fossils or rocks slowly and mindfully. Pause at the various displays, and try to imagine the world as it was when the particular rock or fossil was formed. Put yourself there, and imagine witnessing the living creature, or simply the landscape. Connect with the ancient Earth, and allow yourself to contemplate deep time again and again as you meander around the exhibit halls. If you feel especially creative, bring your journal and write either poetry or prose to help you reflect on the experience. Sketching or drawing is also helpful if you feel artistically inclined.

A variation on this experience is to contemplatively approach walking in or around natural rock formations—anything from canyons to roadside rock cuts. If you decide to do a walking meditation on rough terrain, go extra slowly and be cautious with each step. A walking meditation is not a goal-oriented hike. Meditating in this way gives an entirely different experience than that of a museum, but both are equally valuable.

Large Group—Deep Time Ceremony This is an ideal practice to integrate into a worship service, since a sanctuary space generally has the long aisle needed for the demonstration, but it can also be done in any long hallway, or even outdoors. Measure out a fifty-foot line, representing the approximately five billion years of Earth's history. On this scale, 10 feet represent a billion years, a foot represents 100 million years, and an inch represents a little over 8 million years. Designate one end of the line as representing the formation of the Earth and the other as representing the present. Mark the following major events on the line, and add more if you wish.

~ 3.5 billion years before the present (35 feet from the present day end of the line): earliest life appears in the oceans

~ 3.25 billion years before the present (32½ feet): photosynthesis

~ 1.9 billion years before the present (19 feet): first cells with a nucleus appear

~ 650 million years before the present (6½ feet): first multicelled organisms appear

~ 500 million years before the present (5 feet): earliest land plants

~ 245 million years before the present (2 feet, 5 inches): age of dinosaurs begins

~ 65 million years before the present (approximately 8 inches): age of dinosaurs ends with asteroid impact

~ 3.5 million years before the present (approximately ½ inch): earliest proto-humans appear

~ 100,000 years before the present (approximately 1 millimeter): earliest appearance of modern humans

~ 10,000 years before the present (.1 millimeter): earliest human civilizations, recorded history begins.

What you decide to do from here is up to your group's unique creative process. The following suggestions can inspire you to create a meaningful ceremony for contemplating deep time.

~ Have each member walk the timeline as a contemplative meditation.

~ As part of a service, have one person read aloud each milestone along the line as they walk.

~ Create poetry, songs, and/or stories to celebrate each point on the line and use these as part of a service or ceremony.

~ Position people at events along the line. Walk from the beginning to the present, pausing at each person to hear them describe the significance of the event. You could also do this in reverse, moving back toward the beginning.

Whatever you do, be sure to fully engage your group's creativity, and allow the concept of deep time to become real to you in a meaningful way.

For Reflection

~ How long do you think humanity will endure? What factors might influence this?

~ Does the process of contemplating deep time change the way you think about humanity? About non-human species? If so, how?

~ How does the deep time story differ from other creation stories you may have heard as a child? Are the differences significant? What are they?

~ Consider the concept of ownership in light of deep time. Does it change? If so, how?

FOURTEEN

Across the Wide Universe

The ancients had it easy. To them, the heavens offered guidance for the future and hinted at the will of the gods. The sky told stories of tricksters, heroes, and magical beasts. Whether or not they figured out that the Earth revolved around the sun was somewhat beside the point. What really mattered was that the sky was an open book, put there to be read and interpreted. If we weren't the center of the solar system, surely at least our sun was the center of the universe. It all spun around us, put there just so for our benefit. Comforting, isn't it?

Ironically, we are at the center of the universe—sort of. There really is no one center. Everywhere or nowhere can be the center. The entire thing is expanding like a balloon, and any point on the surface is just as much at the center as any other point. In relation to our galaxy, the Milky Way, we are definitely not in the middle of things. Our sun, which is no different than any other ordinary middle-aged star, is located far out on one of the spiral arms of the galaxy, a sort of galactic backwater in a rather hum-drum neighborhood of stars, with nothing particularly exceptional nearby.

It all began back with the Big Bang. Most people have heard of this term, but somehow it lacks the necessary grandeur. Mathematical cosmologist Brian Swimme calls it the Primordial Flaring Forth, and religious naturalist Connie Barlow calls it the Great Radiance. Regardless of the name, this event is the common thread that connects our planet, sun, and solar system with the rest of what's out there. Ultimately, not only are we kin to every living thing that shares our Earth, we are also kin to nebulae, star clusters, and galaxies. In *The Universe Story*, Brian Swimme explains,

> There was no place in the universe that was separate from the originating power of the universe. Each thing of the universe had its very roots in this realm. Even space-time itself was a tossing, churning, foaming out of the original reality, instant by instant. Each of the sextillion particles that foamed into existence had its root in this quantum vacuum, this originating reality.

Our brains are not wired to fully comprehend what's out there in the wide open spaces. The vastness of it all and our own insignificance in the big picture just don't compute. Just as with the concept of deep time, metaphors and analogies work best. The Earth is an atom in the grain of sand that is our galaxy, on the beach that is the universe. We are a snowflake on Everest, or a raindrop in a thousand oceans. We are very, very small.

And consider those breathtaking images of galaxies, nebulae, and star clusters from the Hubble space telescope. They are so far away that we don't even see them as they are today. The light from them has taken millions of years to reach us. When we look through our lenses, we look into the distant past, seeing the galaxies as they were when that light began its journey through space. Even light from the nearest star, *Alpha Centauri*, takes approximately four years to reach us. If it exploded into a supernova tomorrow, we would not know it for four years.

So we can't live in the fantasy world of the ancients, where the stars are laid out in meaningful patterns, solely for our enlightenment. But in literal, physical terms, we're no different than we were centuries ago. We're still here, on the same precious, blue-green gem we've always lived on. We're still spinning around the sun once a year. We may have lost our inflated ego, but hopefully we've gained some understanding, perspective, and awe.

If we want, we can use this newfound understanding about the immensity of it all and the unity of its common origin to recapture some of the wonder that tends to get lost in our technological age. We can reconnect with the wide-eyed awe that is our birthright as conscious beings. We aren't the center of the universe in the way that we thought before, but we are a part of something so much bigger than we are, something far beyond our petty differences and divisions.

Practices

Sky Watch Go out on a clear night with no moon, as far away from city lights as possible. If you can't get completely away from urban light pollution, try a spot in the shadow of a hill, with the city lights behind you. Forget star charts and constellation wheels. Leave the binoculars and telescopes behind. Don't think too much, just look. Lay down on a blanket on the ground and spend some time gazing into the velvet blackness of the great bowl that is the night sky. Let yourself shrink, and the sky grow as big as you can possibly imagine. Then let it grow a little bigger. Imagine entire galaxies with millions of stars, gathered into clusters of their own. Imagine it all expanding, growing, and pushing out into forever. Imagine that you are suspended in space, and the entire sky is below you. In your mind, let go and fall down into the ocean of the infinite.

Hubble's Gifts Search out, either online or in print, some of the images taken by the Hubble space telescope. Spend some time looking at these as you would look at works of art in a museum. Try to identify a couple images as your favorites. See if one particularly resonates with you. It may have some personal symbolism or meaning for you. Unlike the ancients, who looked for specific messages from the sky, you can create meaning for yourself by relating to the images on your own terms. If you like, write in your journal about the experience.

Drop in the Ocean Get a small bottle and fill it with water. A dropper bottle is ideal. Take your water to a lake, river, or, ideally, an ocean. Mindfully, imagine one molecule of water within your bottle. It is one out of billions of other water molecules. Picture it in your mind, glowing blue-green and beautiful. Now, take your bottle and add a drop (or the smallest amount you can pour) to the lake, river, or ocean. Sit nearby, and meditate for a few minutes on the tiny drop now drifting in the larger body of water, and that beautiful molecule you imagined drifting out with it. Follow its journey in your imagination. Where does it go? Now, mentally make the leap and see the molecule as the Earth, floating in the ocean of the universe. Allow your mind to play with that image for a while before you return to the cares of daily life.

Large Group—Star Party This is simply the "Sky Watch" practice described above, on a larger scale. Ideally, group members will experience both a solitary sky watch and the party with the group. Just like the individual practice, find a dark place away from city lights, and simply experience it all. Choose a night when the moon is new or nearly so. A full moon can render all but the brightest stars invisible. Make it an event—bring blankets, drinks, and snacks. Keep the lights low. Use candles or small lanterns for light, so as not to impede your sky viewing. Avoid large campfires. If you'd like, schedule your party to coincide with a meteor shower. The Perseids arrive every summer and are perfect for viewing with friends. Open up, and share your sense of wonder with others in the group.

For Reflection

~ What are some metaphors or analogies, in addition to those mentioned here, that could describe our place or size in the universe?

~ How do you feel when you consider the vastness of the heavens? What emotions does the experience of staring at the night sky evoke in you?

~ If you're reading this book straight through, consider the concept of deep time from the last chapter, "Deep Time Journeys" (page 77), together with the thoughts from this chapter. Do they seem different in any way when they are considered together as a whole? If so, how?

~ So, what is the meaning of it all? Is there a meaning to existence? Do we create meaning for ourselves, or are there greater forces at work? Does it matter?

FIFTEEN

Becoming Conscious Animals

I once saw a T-shirt that said something like, "You share 25 percent of your genes with a banana. Get over yourself!" It's true. We also share common ancestors with living creatures as diverse as whales, fruit flies, and geckos. Just like you share a common ancestor with your siblings and a slightly more distant one with your cousins, humans share common ancestors with their fellow creatures of the Earth. The connection may be recent, as with chimpanzees, or more distant, as with birds or reptiles, but the connection is real and becoming more and more clear as the science of genetics develops.

Like our knowledge of the universe, our scientific understanding of the connectedness of life is recent in the overall human experience. Its roots go back to Charles Darwin, but it was not fully comprehended even by scientists until the last few decades and the advent of DNA sequencing. Darwin was on the right track, but didn't understand exactly how traits were passed from generation to generation. He had no knowledge of chromosomes, genes, or the molecules that code our genetic heritage. The implications of our new understanding are profoundly spiritual and hint at the possibility of a shift in our perception of ourselves as a species. We find we are not as different from other life forms as we had presumed. We are kin to every living creature on the face of the Earth. We are family. We are one.

This realization is not new to many indigenous cultures, in which people perceived the animals of their land to be their brothers and sisters, and treated them with respect rather than as objects to be exploited and discarded on a whim. In *Wisdom of the Elders*, authors David Suzuki and Peter Knudtson describe indigenous perspectives as holistic, multisensory, and boundless in scope, enveloping the totality of the cosmos. This perception tends to be lacking in Western thought, which instead tends to compartmentalize knowledge and emphasizes differences rather than commonality. What indigenous people knew intuitively, we now know scientifically. The deep truth of interconnectedness and interdependence is clear. While we may comprehend it intellectually, for the most part, our culture hasn't connected with it in a spiritual way.

Not only do we share common ancestors but we have also learned that we carry the story of all life within us. Every cell of our body is like a time capsule, a message in a bottle, from our deep ancestors. The story encoded within the base pair sequence of our DNA is like a song, written slowly, verse by verse, over eons. Our deepest ancestors wrote the original chorus—the basic chemical processes that made everything possible. Later verses of the song spoke of sense organs, backbones, and limbs. Later still, life sang the verses relating to thought and consciousness, spirit and transcendence. Now, finally we are able to read the music score for ourselves.

If we ponder this process of emergent life, we realize that we are deeply embedded in a grand story, an epic tale beyond any we could imagine. We might not be quite center stage as we have imagined ourselves to be, but we are waking up to the beauty of it all. Surely there is spiritual sustenance to be found here—common spiritual ground for us to build upon, with enough wonder and awe for even the most jaded among us. Our task now is to set aside our compartmentalizing and over-intellectualizing, and view life itself in a more holistic fashion, seeing our fellow creatures as kin.

Practices

Shape-shifting Find a quiet place where you will be undisturbed for fifteen to twenty minutes. Choose an animal for the visualization. This should be an animal about which you have some knowledge, rather than one relatively unknown to you. Sit comfortably, and close your eyes. Relax and breathe slowly and deeply, and imagine yourself becoming this animal. Imagine your limbs changing, along with your skin. Now, imagine yourself living as this animal. How do you move? What do you see? What is your world like? Engage all your senses as fully as possible. When you are ready to end the visualization, acknowledge mentally that you are kin to this creature. You share an ancestor in the tree of life, and a common heritage. Breathe consciously, open your eyes, and slowly emerge from your imaginings.

Discover Your Deep Ancestors If you wish to learn more about your particular place in the story of humanity, you can use DNA sequencing to discover some of the story of your ancient ancestors. The Genographic Project supported by the National Geographic Society or companies like Oxford Ancestors will sequence your mitochondrial DNA. This is the DNA that passes unchanged through the maternal line back through tens of thousands of years. From it you can learn where your far-distant grandmother lived and when, and trace her path back to the earliest humans who emerged in Africa millions of years ago. Men can follow the Y-chromosome paternal line as well. The cost of these services has dropped considerably in recent years due to advances in technology. See the "For Further Exploration" section on page 165 for more information.

Mind Map Humans are animals. Spend some time journaling about your own animal nature, emotions, instincts, and desires. Set aside your over-thinking intellect for a while, and let your inner animal speak. What wisdom does it offer? For a change of pace from ordinary journaling, try this: On the center of the page, write the words *inner animal*. Then, create a "mind map" by drawing lines radiating outward, and write other words or short phrases that connect or flow from the original phrase. More words or phrases can flow from these as well. The words can be anything from an emotion, such as *angry*, to a behavior, such as *hibernate*, to the name of a specific animal. Try to write without pausing, as you would during stream-of-consciousness journaling. Allow your thoughts to flow naturally as you fill up the page with words and phrases. Remember, there is no such thing as a "wrong" mind map. When you're finished, look back at the whole page, and see where your thoughts took you. Are there any surprises? A variation on this exercise is to use your non-dominant hand, which sometimes results in fresh perspectives since it utilizes different neural pathways within the brain.

Large Group—Tree of Life Mural A mural is a wonderful group project, and this one can be as simple as taping photos on a wall or as elaborate as a permanent painting in a worship or classroom space. Begin with an image of a bare tree on your wall, and have each participant add images of several animals and/or plants to the branches. Have group members share why they chose the particular animals or plants they did. Be sure to include humans somewhere on the tree.

A variation on this practice—suitable for inclusion in a worship service or ritual—entails creating a symbolic Tree of Life. Use a bare tree branch, either fallen or carefully cut, and create ornaments to hang on it representing the various forms of life on Earth. Group members can add the ornaments as part of a larger worship service. Also, the entire tree can decorate your meeting space.

For Reflection

∽ Evolutionary psychology posits that much of human behavior—such as aggression, food choices, and moral decisions—can be explained by evolutionary forces. What do you think? What are the implications of these ideas for society?

∽ Are there some forms of life, either plant or animal, to which you feel a particular connection or kinship? Why do you think this is so? What does the connection mean to you?

∽ If we think of the Earth as one whole living being, completely interconnected, what role do humans play? Are we the mind of Gaia? The spirit? Or something else entirely?

∽ Why is it difficult for people from industrialized cultures to relate to animals, plants, and the natural world with a sense of spiritual kinship? What is it about contemporary culture that makes this such a challenge?

SIXTEEN

Rare, Precious and Not at All Inevitable

So far, we've situated ourselves as quite small in relation to the big world. In terms of the history of life on Earth, we've come into the story quite recently. In the overall picture of the universe, we are unimaginably tiny. We have so much in common with our fellow species that we may have lost our sense of being anything at all out of the ordinary. If you find yourself experiencing a kind of existential crisis after all that, you've come to the right chapter.

While we are clearly not the *raison d'être* of the universe, all the creatures that populate the Earth today—including ourselves—are indeed quite special. Of all the species that have ever lived, it's estimated that 99 percent have gone extinct. They evolved into being, lived for a time, and then, for one reason or another, perished. Certainly, many have gone extinct from human activity, and this is a tragedy that deserves our attention to prevent more losses. But this is not always the case. Most people are familiar with the catastrophe that led to the extinction of the dinosaurs, but even this is dwarfed by the Permian extinction—also sometimes called the Great Dying—where approximately 90 percent of species went extinct. The survivors went on to repopulate the Earth, evolving new and different forms along the way.

For the moment at least, our species has survived. We are here to tell the tale, which was not a foregone conclusion. We tend to think that the path leading to our emergence was a clear one, a direct chain from the earliest life to us—logical and pre-destined. After all, we're here, aren't we?

Well, yes, we're here. But we certainly weren't inevitable. Evolution is not so much a direct chain as a tangled thicket. Of the dozen or so hominid species within that thicket, we are the only one still here. We are the only one to create masterpieces of art. We are the only one to have written language, and transmit our knowledge across time and space. For that matter, we are the only one to venture out into space, to look back at our home in awe. Biologist and author Ursula Goodenough notes that we are uniquely religious creatures. We need answers to the big existential questions. We need to make sense of our lives, and give ourselves a sense of hope through our belief systems.

So while we might be small in relation to the big picture, we are also rare and precious—a gem indeed. We are incredibly creative and ingenious problem solvers. We are artists, dreamers, poets, scientists, and musicians. We are sons and daughters, mothers and fathers, brothers and sisters, lovers and friends. We have the capacity to feel compassion for each other, and the creatures who share our planet. We are capable of acts of tremendous kindness and deep abiding love. Despite all our problems, we aren't entirely bad. Even so, our unique capacities give us unique responsibilities. Many species that share the Earth with us today are in danger of extinction due to human activity. These too are survivors, just as we are. They too trace their evolutionary history back through the tangled thicket to the beginnings of life. They too are rare and precious gems.

Practices

Many Paths and Possibilities Just as evolution could have taken many other paths than the one it did, our lives also could have turned out differently had we made different choices. Either in your thoughts or in your journal, reflect on the roads not taken in your life. Do not get bogged down in regrets for what might have been a better path. Rather, acknowledge the many possibilities, as well as the path you did choose. Next, consider the many paths open to you at this stage of your life. They may be different from the ones in the past, but life always has choices and possibilities. Consider the analogy that you on your life's path are like a kayaker traveling down a huge river delta toward the sea. Along the way, the kayaker comes to many points where a choice must be made about which branch of the river to take. This process is repeated over and over, leading to the sea. Only one unique path is taken from the many possibilities that exist. So it is with the evolving Earth.

Honoring Your Uniqueness Clear your altar of any previously used items. You are a singular being, unlike anyone else on Earth, now or in the past. Your experiences, perceptions, life story, and genetics are unique. Even if you have an identical twin, your life experiences are yours alone. Express this uniqueness on your altar. Put up some photos of your ancestors to represent your genetic legacy, and some items that symbolize your life story and experiences. This is a creative snapshot of the person you are right now. How might your altar have been different had you created it five years ago? Ten years ago?

Observe Endangered Species Day Sadly, many animals are on the path to extinction due to human activity. Since 2006, environmental groups around the world have commemorated endangered species with a special day, to bring attention to the issue. In the United States, the third Friday of May has been designated as Endangered Species Day. Similar days are observed in other countries such as Australia, on varying dates. Think about ways to mark the day in a meaningful way. Consider participating in a local event, or writing a letter to the editor of your local paper to raise awareness. Learn about some endangered species in your bioregion. Discover how you might help them survive and adapt to a changing world.

Large Group—Memorial for an Extinct Species In every community there are creative ways for people to memorialize their loved ones. For example, plaques can be put on park benches, displaying the names of the deceased. Public gardens can have walkways containing memorial bricks. Church services commonly use altar flowers dedicated to someone's memory. Gather your group, and plan a memorial to extinct species. It can be dedicated to one specific species, or all animals made extinct by human actions. It can be as simple or elaborate, temporary or permanent as your group wishes it to be. Outdoor memorials, or those associated with a park or nature preserve, are particularly appropriate. One example includes a gift of several birdhouses made by group members for endangered birds on a nature trail. Or the group might plant some native wildflowers. You may choose to mark the gift with an explanatory plaque, or leave it unadorned. If you prefer not to create a permanent memorial, consider hosting an event for Endangered Species Day (see above exercise) and incorporating a tribute to extinct species as part of the event. Some groups may be uncomfortable memorializing a non-human species; others may embrace the idea. As always, make your project suit your particular group and its uniqueness. Respect the feelings of group members.

For Reflection

∾ Not only are we rare and precious, but so are the other creatures that share the Earth with us. What obligation, if any, do we have to the other living beings on our planet?

∾ How can we balance human needs with the needs of other species who also call the Earth home?

∾ Imagine a world where more than one hominid species survived to the present day. What might that world be like? What challenges would people face while sharing the world with our very close cousins? How would we define human?

∾ What are some positive traits of the human species? Negative ones? How can we balance the two?

SEVENTEEN

Reality?

Warning: The topics and practices presented in this chapter have been known to cause states of radical amazement, head-scratching befuddlement, and the sudden desire to watch old *Star Trek* episodes.

So, what are you made of? Sugar and spice? 60 percent water? Bone and muscle? How about open space? So far, on the path of discovery, we've mostly concerned ourselves with the macro, visible world—stuff we can see. For the most part, this macro world makes logical sense. Parts fit together nicely into wholes, and we experience moments of clarity and understanding.

What we are about to discuss here is a different animal entirely. Logic that serves us well in the macro-scale world falls to pieces. Reality turns out to be far more bizarre than we had previously imagined—and far more amazing too. So, back to the question: What are you made of? Mostly nothingness, actually. Open space. You are made of tissues composed of cells that contain molecules made up of atoms. And atoms, it turns out, are mostly made of nothing. If you imagine a grain of rice lying in the middle of Times Square, the rice represents the nucleus of the atom and the rest of Times Square represents the space in which the electrons of that atom exist. The rice and the open space together represent the entire atom. So, if all matter consists of atoms made up of mostly nothingness, we hold entire universes of open space within our being. Our perception of solidity, of ourselves as discrete entities is an illusion. At the atomic level, there is no boundary, no division between you and the rest of the universe. It's mostly open space. Sort of.

Physicists now believe that all this open space isn't quite so empty after all. It's frothing with energy and virtual particles that flit into and out of existence constantly. Being and non-being. Existence and nothingness. The luminous void. It exists within each of us, all the time. Moving out to the really big macro scale, outer space isn't quite so empty either. The possibilities of dark energy and dark matter are throwing monkey wrenches into our understanding of the universe. The implications of our new understanding of reality both at the subatomic and intergalactic scales are overflowing with majesty and wonder. This is Mystery, with a capital M. Some might call it Holy, Sacred Mystery. Author Barbara Fiand notes that mystics from both Eastern and Western religious traditions have consistently advised us "not to confuse *our* reality with *the* reality—Ultimate Reality, which, in fact ever remains Mystery." Wise advice. This Mystery transcends religious boundaries and human divisions, including the divide between those who call themselves religious and those who do not.

Mystery itself seems to be built into the fabric of the universe. Physicist Werner Heisenberg's uncertainty principle explains that it is impossible to know both the velocity and location of any given particle with any precision. Knowing one changes the other. There is always an unknown. Even more bizarre is the fact that the observer even affects the existence of the observed. If all this isn't enough for you, toss in the possibility of multiple universes, eleven (or more) dimensions on top of the four we experience, the curvature of space time, and a little relativity just for fun. Are you boggled yet?

Even the most brilliant physicists in the world don't have all this figured out. For the average person, considering these ideas can be a journey into awe and wonder, which alone is a worthwhile thing. The exercises below offer suggestions for simply playing around with the mysteries of the universe, and spiritually stretching into truly magical territory. Don't confuse them with actual science, but do feel free to go watch a few episodes of *Star Trek*.

Practices

Unity Visualization This is one of my personal favorites, and I find it to be quite soothing in stressful times. Sit comfortably in a place where you will be undisturbed for fifteen minutes or so. Start out looking at your hand. See the texture of your skin, and imagine that you are looking at it through a microscope, closer and closer, deeper into the layers. It's helpful to close your eyes at this point. Visualize seeing your skin in close detail, and slowly increase the magnification of your imaginary microscope. Now you can see your cells. Pick one, and go closer. You can see the nucleus and all the organelles working in harmony. Look closely at the nucleus, and go in closer there. You can see your chromosomes and then your DNA, that part of you that makes you who you are. Go in closer still, and see the twisted ladder of the double helix. You are so close now that you begin to see fuzzy atoms. Go closer. You see open space, and the tiny nucleus of an individual atom. Imagine this space filled with virtual particles flitting into and out of existence. Moving closer, you see the protons and neutrons of the nucleus. How do they look to you? Looking closer still, you see the quarks. How do they look? As you observe them, you notice them slowly changing, and a star takes their place. Backing out a bit, you now see a galaxy, then another. Stay here for a while. See the harmony of it all, the beauty. When you are ready, come back to the present, and slowly open your eyes. If you wish, reflect on your experience in your journal.

The Unknowable Path If you've not already done the "Many Paths and Possibilities" practice (page 99), go back and do it now. After you complete the exercise, look at what you wrote. As you review the paths you didn't take, reflect on the idea that the outcomes you presume from any given path are in reality unknowable. For example, you might have written something like, "If only I had done _____, I would be happier today." As you look back at your outcomes, imagine a different one. If you had done that action that you wrote about, it may not have turned out the way you imagined. How else could it have been? Try to picture several scenarios. Maybe it would be better than you envisioned, maybe worse. But it is unknowable. It is your personal Mystery. With a spirit of gentleness toward yourself, release all the possibilities, let go of any regrets, and spend some time writing about the unknowns in your own life.

Shape of the Unknown Consider the mysterious virtual particles and mysterious energies that physicists believe exist in the open spaces within an atom—and you—the ones that come into being only to blip back into oblivion again. How do you imagine them? Do they hold any meaning for you? Using this most ephemeral aspect of reality as your muse, simply create. Using any media that you like—sculpture, painting, or even dance—create your vision of this unknown, yet oddly intimate aspect of your world. As you create, call to mind the fact that all this Mystery resides within you at this very moment.

Large Group—Unity Visualization Try the "Unity Visualization," described above, with a few enhancements for your group. Have everyone bring a comfortable cushion or pillow. Participants can sit in a traditional cross-legged meditative pose, lie down, or even sit in a comfortable chair. Begin the session by playing some soft, relaxing music that can play through the entire session if desired. Allow participants to settle in, slowly breathe, and relax for several minutes before beginning. The leader should then slowly guide the group through the visualization, allowing time at each new level of imagining. Afterward, gently guide the group back to the present moment. Pause, and then allow participants to stretch and move a little before sharing their perceptions of the experience with each other.

For Reflection

～ The subatomic, molecular, microscopic, and macroscopic worlds all exist simultaneously. How do they differ? How does what we call reality depend on what world is being considered? Is one more real than another?

～ How does the macro (ordinary perceived) world relate to the others? Do the problems we perceive in the everyday world have any relevance or meaning at these other levels of reality?

～ How do the implications of modern physics fit together—or not—with religious traditions and ways of understanding the world? Do some traditions blend with these implications more easily than others? How so?

～ At the atomic level and beyond the division between you and what is not you falls away. Only a continuum of particles exists. Does this change how you perceive and relate to your world and others in it? How?

EIGHTEEN

Transformation

Here we are—tiny and insignificant, yet unique and precious. This is true both for us as individuals and for the human race as a whole. We are caught up in the grand story that is the universe, swept along by forces of creation and dissolution, being and nothingness, life and death, always moving toward the future in ways that are beyond our control. Sooner or later, we all die. For us as sentient, conscious beings with the capacity to consider our own future deaths, the realization of this truth can be troubling.

Even a cursory glance at the natural world leads one to the inevitable conclusion of the necessity of death. Without it, there would simply be no room for new life. Looking a little deeper, we see that death and decay are integral to life itself. The leaves that fall in autumn provide nutrients for the green shoots that emerge in the spring. Predator devours prey. The dance of "I eat you, you eat me" goes on. Thousands of neurons in a newborn's brain die in order for others to form connections. Without these cell deaths, the child's development would be impaired. Even deaths that seem unnatural are part of the cycle. The fox finds the mother rabbit's burrow. The baby zebra ends up in the lion's mouth. The eggs grow cold from exposure and never hatch. The fawn simply cannot find enough to eat. In the not-so-distant past, it was commonplace for a child to die before age five. It may not be easy or pretty but it is natural. Death, like life, simply is.

Even on the grandest scale of all, death is integral. Every atom in your body had its beginnings inside a massive ancient star that exploded. On the early Earth, the evolution of new complex forms of life that ultimately led to the evolution of humanity necessitated the death or extinction of other forms. Life flows onward, creating and expanding anew. But so does death. Death flows onward, cleansing, clearing, recycling, providing the raw materials for life processes. Death cannot exist without life, but life cannot exist without death. They are so intimately intertwined that they are really best considered as one process. Our language does not have a word for such a process. Perhaps the most useful word is *transformation*, since both life and death are continuous processes of transformation and change. *Transformation* also doesn't carry the negative baggage associated with the word *death*. We—and everything else that exists—are always in the process of being, becoming, dissolving, evolving, transforming.

If we imagine all that is—the entire dynamic being of the universe over all of time—as an ocean, then each of our individual lives is like a single wave. We come into and out of our individual existence, but are never separated from the larger whole. Of course, that whole can be named in any number of ways: the Ground of All Being, Goddess, God, All That Is, Universe, Source, the Divine, and more.

Practices

Transformation Clear your altar, and collect items that fall into two broad categories: alive and formerly alive. Examples of living things could include a potted plant or a small fish tank. Formerly alive items might include feathers, bones, dried leaves, or seashells. Arrange them to suit you, and leave them in place for a week or so. Spend some time daily at your altar considering the following:

∾ How are the items you categorize as alive in the process of transforming into something you would not consider alive?

∾ How are the items you categorize as not alive in the process of transforming into something you would consider alive?

∾ On what sort of timescale might these transformations play out—weeks, years, centuries? Does this influence how you think about the items or categories?

Imagine Your Own Funeral Note: if you are depressed or have struggled with thoughts of suicide, consult a mental health professional before doing this exercise, or just skip it entirely. Assuming this is not the case, spend some time imagining what your funeral will be like. In your journal, explore how you wish it would be and how you would like to be remembered by family and friends. In your imagination, is it a quiet memorial or a rowdy wake? Is there any particular music playing or poems someone is reading? Who is there?

If you wish, consider pre-planning services offered by many funeral homes. You can plan, pay for, and make choices for your own funeral. This would help ensure that your wishes are carried out, and also spare family members from having to make these decisions during their time of grief.

Life Cycle Project Even if you garden regularly, try the following for an ongoing contemplative experience. Follow the life cycle of a plant from seed to seed. Choose an easy-to-grow flowering annual plant, such as a marigold or zinnia. Pick a variety that is relatively short and suitable for growing in a pot, in case you need to move it indoors for frost protection. Plant your seed in a pot. As you do so, mindfully consider the seed as a metaphor for the life/death/rebirth transformation cycle. Water it, tend it, place it in a sunny location, and watch it grow. If possible, an excellent spot for your plant is an outdoor altar. When it flowers, don't "deadhead" it by removing the blooms to encourage more blooms. Instead, allow the plant to complete its natural life cycle. Monitor it as it goes to seed, and eventually dies. Allow it to completely transform by simply leaving it in its pot, and observe as the plant gradually becomes part of the soil itself, ready to grow the next generation. If you're lucky, some of the seeds may sprout into that next generation, and you can observe all over again. Obviously, this is an ongoing project that will take many months. Throughout this time, reflect on the process in your journal, and allow the flower to inspire your own thoughts and ideas.

Large Group—Examining the Culture Gather as a large group, and share experiences. Our contemporary culture denies death, and tries to postpone it as long as possible regardless of the quality of life. Share experiences related to how our culture handles serious illness, impending death, funeral rituals, and grief. Share openly and honestly, but respectfully, realizing that although we share a culture, our individual stories and experiences are unique.

For Reflection

~ Is there such a thing as a "good death"? If so, describe it.

~ How might reframing the concepts of life and death into the broader concept of transformation alter how we think about them?

~ How can a nature-based, deep-time perspective help us through the grieving process? Can it be blended into traditional religious beliefs? If so, how? If not, why?

~ Consider the entire life/death/transformation cycle from the perspective of a mountain, a town, a civilization/culture, a language, a bacterium, an insect, or any other entity. Be sure to place them in the larger context of the story of the universe.

IV

The Path of Creation

After grounding ourselves and discovering our place in the grand scheme of things, we've arrived at the path of creation. It's here that we put our new understanding to work, and begin to envision and create a new way of being, a new personal paradigm. Then we can stretch our wings and create new possibilities for our culture and our world.

In this process, we envision the sort of life and world that we want for ourselves and others. We contemplate the changes we must make to move us closer to our dreams and visions for the world. From small, personal decisions to global change, the path of creation belongs to the here and now, as well as to the future. It's time to get started creating a mindful, meaningful, and joyful life. It's time to create a new global paradigm to heal the Earth.

NINETEEN

EveryDay Sacred

Somewhere along the line, most of us pick up the idea that certain times or places are simply more holy than others. It's not surprising. We all have places we consider to be extra special, and there's nothing wrong with that. There's no doubt that cathedrals and mountaintops are extraordinary places, and that meditative retreat weekends are special times. But when we begin to internalize that those times and places are somehow intrinsically more sacred than the stuff of our everyday lives, we run into problems. The difference about holy places and times is our awareness and expectation of a spiritual experience. When we walk through a Zen garden, its quiet beauty acts on our mind, and settles us into a more peaceful state. Because of our expectations—"this is a holy place, pay attention"—our subconscious subtly shifts, and we find ourselves open to the experience of the Sacred. We expect the experience, and most of the time we have it. If we don't, we may leave the sacred place feeling disappointed and a little depressed.

The problem is that most of our lives are not lived in Zen gardens, or medieval cathedrals, or remote wilderness areas. We do not spend the majority of our time in quiet contemplation or divine ecstatic bliss. We live most of our lives in very ordinary places, where we spend our time doing very ordinary things. We care for our kids, go to work, pay the bills, cook dinner, mow the lawn, watch the news, and so on. If we set up the expectation that the Sacred is something remote from us, something "out there," far removed from nitty-gritty reality, then it's no wonder we flop into our beds every night wondering why life isn't more fulfilling.

As we move onto the path of creation, we begin to envision how we can live sustainable, Earth-honoring lives. As we let go of the destructive paradigms of contemporary culture, we consider how to live in a way that honors our deepest values and our place in the grand scheme of life.

Every . . . day . . . sacred. Everyday sacred. EveryDay sacred. We don't need more time up on the mountaintop, however pleasant that might be. We need to grow our awareness of the Holy that surrounds us, and infuses us every moment of our lives. This is the case regardless of how we conceptualize the Holy. All of us need to cultivate a way of being in the world that satisfies our human longing to connect with something greater than ourselves, and to situate our individual lives within the story of all life.

Back in chapter 13, "Deep Time Journeys" (page 77), we used the analogy of a football field to conceptualize when humanity emerged on the Earth. Remember that if one end zone represents the beginnings of life on Earth, humans wouldn't appear until near the edge of the other end zone. As we work with that analogy a little more and consider all the life that came before us, we realize that of all the beings, both human and nonhuman, that have ever called planet Earth their home, we are unique. Each of us has singular experiences and life journeys that are not duplicated by any of the myriad of beings that have ever lived. The life that you are living is totally unique in the history of the universe. This life is a one-of-a-kind spark of consciousness in the grand epoch that is all existence. Every day, every breath, every moment. Sacred. Unique.

When this realization dawns on us, we are struck with the overwhelming holiness of it all. We live in this state of grace every day of our lives. Our task is to continually move in the direction of ever-increasing awakening. In the end, it really is all good. It is all holy. Poet Gunilla Norris, in her book *Being Home*, contemplates the sacredness of everyday experiences. Pondering the simple act of walking across a wooden floor, she writes, "When I walk I am walking on the wood and in the woods. I am walking on the life of these trees." Walking becomes a devotional act, filled with reverence. The Sacred has permeated the mundane.

The question now becomes how to move toward awakening this awareness in the midst of the daily grind. Consciousness of the Sacred is not a goal that is ever permanently achieved. It is not a static state of being. Some days we will be more conscious than others. That's real life. The process of moving in the direction of awakening is itself holy, dynamic, and fluid. If the Sacred is infinite, then the movement never ends. There is no end state, only the process of awakening, and then awakening some more.

Folk singer and songwriter Peter Mayer sings, "God is a river, swimmer, so let go." It's true. We are all like fish, swimming in the ocean of the Divine every moment of our lives, unaware of the water that surrounds us and gives us life. But we can awake to the existence of the water. Feel it moving all around, sometimes fast, like rapids, other times a slow flow. Wake up, swimmer.

Practices

EveryDay Sacred Altar Decorate your altar with items symbolic of your daily life, such as a grocery receipt, bus pass, pen, child's toy (one that your child is not emotionally attached to), bar of soap, or calculator. If you travel frequently for your job, perhaps select a baggage claim tag. If you cook your family's meals, maybe a wooden spoon would work. Choose your items with care. Arrange them with intention. Perhaps use an altar cloth. Then, place a candle on the altar. Light the candle, and think about what you've created, and how you spend your days.

Small Miracles This practice is best done on a regular basis, over a lifetime, but today is as good a day as any to begin. In the course of your ordinary tasks, pause for a minute. Take a deep, slow breath. Then bring your awareness to any number of small miracles that take place around you all the time. Small miracles include breath itself, a bird perched on a fence, a sleeping baby, autumn leaves, an earthworm, conscious thought, a starry night and eyes to see it, flowing water, dreaming, the ground under your feet. Take a moment to ponder. Take a moment to wonder. Take another deep, slow breath, and then return to your day. Ideally, considering these small miracles should become a daily practice, a brief pause that grounds and refreshes us in the middle of the everyday routine. If you find that you have trouble remembering to pause, leave yourself a reminder in the form of a sticky note, a touchstone in your pocket, or even setting your watch alarm to beep occasionally. After a while, you won't need the prompts.

Ordinary Outdoors Those of us who are ecologically conscious tend to focus much of our attention and donation dollars on saving endangered species and habitats. This is necessary and absolutely worthwhile, but so much focus on the rare and exotic can blind us to the wisdom of common creatures that inhabit our lives and backyards. Go to your own backyard or a nearby park and spend some time observing the animal and plant residents. Sit quietly so you don't disturb them more than necessary. Observe their activities and whether they are aware of your presence. Watch how they interact with each other. Observe plants as well as animals, see what you learn. Take them as your teachers. What wisdom can they offer you? After a period of observation time, write in your journal about your experience.

Large Group—EveryDay Sacred Gather in a large circle, and take turns sharing sacred moments from your own daily lives. These can be regular occurrences, or one-time moments. Save the mountaintop special experiences for another time. Right now, just focus on ordinary life and the pleasures it brings. Afterward, spend about fifteen minutes in silent meditation together, simply breathing slowly and deeply while bringing your attention to the present moment. This can be done sitting in chairs, sitting on the floor, or even lying down. Use a sound cue such as a bell, singing bowl, or even recorded music to bring the group back from the quiet meditative state.

For Reflection

∿   Is there a special place that feels sacred or holy? What makes it special?

∿   Are there times in your daily life that invite connection to the greater whole? Perhaps early morning when everyone else is still asleep or maybe even a commute over a quiet country road? What feels special to you?

∿   How can you cultivate a sense of the sacred amid everyday problems and challenges? What personal rituals or practices might help you do this?

∿   If you knew you would die tomorrow, how would you view today?

TWENTY

Facing, Embracing, Transcending

Our evolutionary legacy is a mixed bag. On one hand, we have unwanted impulses like cravings for sugary, fatty foods. These desires served our ancestors well in the eons before the invention of donuts, but now they undermine our health and well-being. Our aggressive tendencies and fight-or-flight adrenaline responses are other examples of traits that served us in the past but are not well suited for modern life. Call them the shadow side of our evolutionary history. On the other hand, we evolved brains powerful enough to begin to unlock the mysteries of the universe. We perform astonishing medical miracles and enjoy a level of mobility unheard of in past centuries. We also have leanings toward intimacy, social order, and cooperation. We are complicated creatures, full of paradoxes. Our species is incredibly violent, yet capable of compassion and tenderness. We can be selfish and greedy, but also generous and self-sacrificing. The key questions are: What aspects of our humanity does our culture reward? What is suppressed? What is encouraged? The answers determine the kind of world we create.

Evolutionary thinker and theologian Michael Dowd has re-conceptualized the notion of original sin. We all struggle with aspects of our nature that undermine our best intentions. Dowd says that this is a manifestation of the shadow side of our evolutionary legacy. By recognizing this part of our nature for what it is, we can understand our less desirable impulses, learn to manage (but not completely eliminate) them, and become more compassionate in the process. This is necessary for us to move forward as individuals and as a species. Not only should we face up to our shadow side, but we also need to embrace the parts of our nature that can help us create a sustainable future.

Not surprisingly, we also find that we are evolutionarily programmed to respond to the natural world. Time spent in nature is healing and can help us tap into the better angels of our nature. Dr. Howard Clinebell, author of *Ecotherapy: Healing Ourselves, Healing the Earth*, notes, "An unexpected psychological benefit from intimate bonding with nature is the awakening of creative mental processes. . . . It enlivens the dance between the functions of the right and left hemispheres of the brain. This playful dance is the essential generator of creativity." Healing our world and healing ourselves are deeply intertwined.

We are community builders, creative problem solvers, tool makers, gentle nurturers, and curious explorers. All these traits can serve us well as we realign ourselves toward an Earth-healing lifestyle. We are not inherently and entirely bad, as some religious ideologies would lead us to believe, but neither are we inherently and entirely good, as some fluffy new-age gurus would declare. We are both shadow and light, and it is up to us which aspects of our nature we choose to nurture.

As helpful as it may be to nurture such evolved human tendencies as our ability to create loving community, this alone is not enough. To address global problems and begin to heal the damage our species has inflicted on the Earth, we need to transcend our limited vision, and see the big picture. We have evolved to perceive and act in response to immediate, physical, local threats. If we are attacked by a wild animal, we are programmed to respond. If we didn't, we would perish. However, the threats to our well-being nowadays come not from a wild animal attack but from invisible sources like toxic pollutants in our air and water, climate change, or over-population.

To create healthy communities, and to heal ourselves as individuals and as a society, approach the problem in three ways: face up to the dark side of our evolutionary legacy, embrace and build upon the helpful aspects of our evolved nature, and transcend the aspects of our evolutionary heritage that limit our vision. Call it Facing, Embracing, and Transcending—the three point plan for creating the future. There is so much to do. We'd better get busy.

Practices

The Shadow Knows In your journal, choose one aspect of what you consider to be the shadow side of your nature and explore it in light of your evolutionary legacy. This could be something like an addiction, an unhealthy habit, or even a bad temper. Try to relate your issue today to the survival of your ancient ancestors, both human and non-human. Look for the mismatch between what might have been helpful in the past and what is now problematic. For example, a quick, knee-jerk aggressive response may have helped fend off an attack from a predator. Now, it only gets you in trouble. Today highly addictive substances exist in concentrations that used to be virtually unknown in the natural world. In the past, substances that provoked good feelings, such as a full stomach, were associated with good things, like finding enough food. Our brains and bodies are ill equipped to handle the highly addictive chemicals that are now available to us. Examine your life, and your shadow, in as much detail as you wish. You may want to go slowly and revisit this topic several times in order to fully explore it.

Love's Legacy We are biologically programmed to connect deeply with others in a loving, intimate way. Loving feelings literally influence our brains, producing chemicals called endorphins that enhance our health. Create a collage of photos of the people who have loved you the most deeply over the course of your life, and those whom you most deeply love. Do not place a photo in your collage out of a sense of obligation—such as a picture of a relative, perhaps. Rather, focus on those people with whom you have a soul-deep connection, regardless of biological relationships. Of course, for many, biological and soul connections will go hand in hand. As with all practices, there is no wrong way to express yourself.

Your collage can be a temporary one of photos placed on a table or your altar that lasts only a day or so, or you can create a framed permanent version to hang on a wall to remind you of those who have blessed your life with love.

The Visible and the Invisible This is an exercise in active observation. Find a place, preferably outside, where you can sit undisturbed for at least twenty minutes. For the first ten minutes or so, pay attention to your surrounding environment using your five senses. See what can you learn about your immediate environment from them. Think about how this information might help you find out what you need to know in order to live and thrive. Next, brainstorm all the aspects of your immediate environment that you cannot see. Think of things like air quality, radiation, and more. Consider how these things affect your well-being. Expand your thought now, and think globally. From where you sit, what aspects of the big picture of the Earth might affect you personally but can't be perceived with your senses? This might include such things as changing weather patterns, or diminishing stocks of ocean fish. Finally, focus your attention back to your immediate environment and spend another minute or two observing it again. Has anything changed in the time it took to do this exercise? If you wish, reflect on your experiences in your journal or discuss them with a friend.

Large Group—Cultivating Community Gather your group together for a potluck dinner for the sole purpose of enjoying each other's company. This event should have no other agenda. No seriousness allowed! What sort of evening would your group enjoy? Perhaps dinner and dancing—have someone bring a boom box and some old disco tunes. Maybe a game night would suit your group better, or a picnic with a campfire afterward.

Later at home, participants should actively reflect on the time spent just having fun with the group. Consider these questions: How do experiences like this one help cement a community together? How might they help foster the creation of truly sustainable communities in the future? Next time the group gathers, share reflections.

For Reflection

∾ How can we as a species transcend our evolutionary programming in order to address the challenges that face us on a global scale?

∾ How can we reframe global challenges and present them to the public in a way that is in harmony with our evolutionary programming?

∾ Think about the lifestyle of prehistoric hunter-gatherers, and then about our contemporary lifestyle. Where are the mismatches? What behaviors, desires, or traits served our forbears well but cause us problems today? How can we address these problems?

∾ What aspects of human nature do you consider to be good or bad? Would the categories be different if our circumstances were different?

TWENTY-ONE

Slow Life

One thing almost all of us seem to have in common, regardless of the details of our lives, is that we are all really busy and really tired! There are an awful lot of people out there who live in a perpetual state of fatigue, trying to balance the various obligations and duties of their lives. They never get enough sleep, much less enough time to relax and savor the pleasures of life. Sound familiar? Even if it doesn't describe you, chances are it describes someone you know. We all know how the fast pace of contemporary life pushes people into overwork and exhaustion. It is as though we keep trying to exhale, by giving our time and energy, without pausing to inhale, by replenishing ourselves.

Humanity evolved in a world without clocks, schedules, or artificially imposed deadlines. We are biologically wired to respond to the daily and seasonal rhythms of light and dark. Women of reproductive age are also unconsciously attuned to the cycle of the moon. The circumstances in which we live today are completely alien to us, biologically speaking. We are ill-equipped to handle the myriad incessant demands and pressures that pull on us from all sides. They act on us as constant low-level stressors, raising our blood pressure and giving us indigestion. Considering all we are faced with, it's frankly a miracle that we cope as well as we do.

Author Waverly Fitzgerald, in her book *Slow Time: Recovering the Natural Rhythm of Life*, explains the concept of tempo. A bustling big city has a fast tempo, filled with the frenetic energy of people rushing here and there. A small rural town might have a much slower one, resulting in daily life feeling more relaxed. Tempo is an important concept that illustrates that how we feel about the pace of our lives is influenced not only by our own individual schedules and daily activities but also by our surroundings. Urban dwellers might have to consciously search for an oasis of calm, such as a park or cathedral, in order to really slow down mentally and spiritually, a challenge not faced by those who live in more relaxed surroundings.

The path of creation is all about re-imagining and re-creating our individual lives, as well as acting as a positive force to transform our culture. Unlike the path of awakening, this is mostly a very pleasant, if not entirely easy, process. It also has far grander implications than are apparent at first glance. Healing the Earth and creating a sustainable world is a daunting prospect. It seems too big and abstract, and just not possible. But stop for a moment and imagine what a sustainable culture might look like. Picture a restored Earth, where humans serve and support the greater whole of the biosphere that ultimately sustains us all. Think about the sort of lifestyle the people live. Are they perpetually exhausted, stressed, and subsisting on fast food, or are they living at a healthier, calmer pace?

Every time one person or one family takes steps to slow down, to reclaim a healthier and more natural life pace, the world moves steadily toward sustainability since healthy, natural, slow-life choices tend also to be environmentally friendly choices. The impact spreads throughout their circle of friends and family. Gradually, the idea of living life slowly and meaningfully begins to catch on. Not only that, but the effect on the individual or family is palpable, and the overall quality of life increases.

As usual, the devil is in the details. As we discussed back in chapter 5, "Cogs in the Machine" (page 25), we are embedded within larger systems over which we have little control. Even so, there are aspects of our lives that we can control. We can choose to slow down. We can say no to one more committee obligation, and in so doing learn to tend to our personal boundaries. We can choose to simply stay home and hang out with our families, instead of rushing off to be entertained elsewhere. We can eat real food. We can turn hanging the laundry outdoors to dry into a kind of meditation. We can find a way to bring a slower pace to our days. We can take a step toward sustainability. We can begin to heal the Earth—and make no mistake, slowing down is an Earth-healing choice.

Practices

Breathing the Hours As part of their religious discipline, medieval monks would pray seven times a day, pausing at regular intervals from dawn to midnight to "pray the hours," using psalms and other texts for their worship. Contemporary Muslims pause for prayer five times daily. Whether modern or medieval, traditions such as these call one away from the flow of ordinary life and create a brief liminal space amid daily tasks. Breathing the hours is a simple way to slow the frantic pace that drives us onward faster and faster. Choose how many times you would like to pause. You can honor an established tradition, such as the monastic hours, or you can create one of your own. Plan to pause at least four times per day. When you pause, go to a window and look out at the sky, trees, flowers, or the like. If you are outdoors, even better. Focus on some aspect of nature around you. Very slowly, take at least five deep breaths. Allow your shoulders to drop and your belly to expand as you breathe. If you find you're having trouble remembering to pause, set your watch alarm or cell phone to remind you. Try to keep up the practice for at least a week, then re-evaluate and continue as you like.

Slow Down Dinner Together with friends or family, plan and cook a meal entirely from scratch, without so-called time saving devices. Don't buy the bagged salad. Buy lettuce from the farmer's market instead. Skip the canned beans; soak and cook the dried variety. Bake bread, peel carrots, slice and dice, knead and mix, all by hand. No electric appliances allowed—with the possible exception of the oven. Use a tablecloth, and cloth napkins. Turn it into a festive experience for all. If there is one regular cook in your household, make sure that he or she is not managing this meal alone. Make it a community project, with all eaters pitching in to help with the cooking. The more, the merrier! Wash the dishes in the sink, not the dishwasher. Play some of your favorite music, and have a leisurely conversation as you eat. For many who are overscheduled, this may take some planning. That's okay. Plan ahead, write it on the calendar, and do it.

Afterward, reflect on the experience. How do you feel now that it's over? How did the meal differ from a more typical one? If you like, plan to eat a slow down dinner on a regular basis. If you can't manage it weekly, try it once a month. The point is not to cause yourself more stress by trying to achieve some "from scratch" standard but instead to help you shift into a slower mode of being. If the food isn't perfect, who cares? Have fun.

Conveniences That Aren't Walk around every room of your house, and take note of any technology that didn't exist one hundred years ago. Then, go back over your list, and evaluate how each device affects your life. If a device is supposed to be a time-saver, evaluate the truth of that claim. Also, consider those devices that seem to suck up large quantities of time and/or money without offering much in return. How do they affect the overall quality of your life? Now, look at the big picture, and consider making any needed changes. Decide which technologies are necessary for your life and which add to the quality of your life. Identify those that are more trouble than they're worth. Adjust your home accordingly.

Large Group—Looking at Time If your group is very large, break into smaller groups of ten or fewer participants. Otherwise, this practice can be done as one group. Sit in a large circle with two white boards or large sheets of paper where everyone can see them. Allow group members to share aspects of their lives that seem rushed or stressed. Write these on the first board. Next, brainstorm ideas that might offer creative ways to address the issues brought up by the group. Write these on the second board. Have participants offer ideas to each other. When we are in the middle of our own busy lives, and caught up in our own frantic pace, we often can't see how to change. We get stuck in a rut. Sharing insights into each others' lives can help us see possibilities we might not see on our own. Consider holding a follow-up session to see how participants have adopted any suggestions from this exercise.

For Reflection

∾ What aspects of modern work life encourage an ever-faster pace? How can we counter these without risking our jobs?

∾ How are our children affected by the high-pressure, fast pace of society? Are they overscheduled? How are they affected by the pressures their parents face?

∾ The essay above describes the connection between slowing down and sustainable living. What other aspects of daily life might also show this connection? What can we do to not only help ourselves live healthier lives, but also affect the Earth?

∾ What does technology have to do with slowing down? How have the various electronic devices in our lives affected our experience of time? Do we perceive time differently because of technology? If so, how?

TWENTY-TWO

Meeting the Soul's Needs

A lifetime spent eating bacon double cheeseburgers will likely end in a triple bypass. We all know this, and yet cheeseburgers still sell quite well, as a trip to any fast food joint will prove. Somewhere deep down in our brains, we are hardwired to crave what the cheeseburger offers—fat and salt. To our ancestors, consuming adequate amounts of fat provided a (literal) cushion to survive times of deprivation. Adequate salt kept our electrolytes in balance. The trouble today comes from the fact that modern food habits have turned evolution on its head. In order to eat a healthy diet now, we need to rethink our inborn cravings, and consciously avoid the junk. Of course, this is not always easy, but when we do eat a healthy diet, we find that we feel a lot better, and we're far less likely to have that bypass.

Something similar has happened to us on psychological and spiritual levels. Just as we are wired to crave fatty foods, we are also wired for companionship, community, love, a positive self-esteem, and the respect of our peers. Psychotherapist Chellis Glendinning combines these needs with a need to connect with the natural world to form what she calls our "Primal

Matrix"—our natural state of being, where all these deep needs are met. Scientists are just beginning to recognize that humans may also be predisposed to spirituality, and that various parts of the brain are unusually active during heightened states of meditation or prayer. It appears that wanting to connect to something greater than oneself is as natural as craving salt. The trouble is that just as junk food turns our natural food desires into a liability, so our culture turns our psychological and spiritual propensities into lifestyles that are unhealthy for us and for the Earth. When we substitute hours of watching so-called reality TV for genuine relationships and community, it's no wonder we feel isolated and lonely. When consumerism dominates society and when status is determined not by one's generosity and service but by one's possessions, the Earth suffers, as we extract ever more resources to meet the demand. Consumerism and media overload are junk food for the spirit, and just as unhealthy. When we struggle to keep up with an ever-faster pace of activity, never pausing to gaze at a sunset or daydream in the shade of a favorite tree, our soul languishes. We have lost our connection to that Primal Matrix. Although for the most part we aren't consciously aware of it, we are still affected by it on a very deep and pervasive level.

The solution is clear. Just as we must consciously choose to eat well and exercise to meet our body's needs, we also must choose to meet our soul's needs. This means mindfully stepping back from the dominant messages of our dysfunctional society and making changes that move us toward a spiritually healthier, more soulful way of life. This process is far from automatic. We are so removed from our natural state of being that for most of us, rediscovering and reintegrating some fragment of the Primal Matrix requires significant effort. The good news is that when we do change, it doesn't just improve our health and happiness; it is also better for the Earth, since we begin to change how we relate to the Earth. Meeting the needs of our souls primarily involves relationships with our inner selves, each other, and the natural world.

In our culture, we pay lip service to valuing relationships, but our actions speak louder than our words. A thousand different demands pull on us in all directions, and it's easy to allow those who matter most to slip further down on our list. We need to place clear boundaries on our time and energy to protect what really matters. Prioritizing relationships with the people who are the most important to us may involve something as simple as eating dinner as a family more often—or something as major as downsizing to a less expensive home. It is no coincidence that simpler lifestyle choices both improve interpersonal connections and also help heal the Earth. A simpler lifestyle means less consumption and less strain on natural resources. For example, consider the choice to spend a family night at home hanging out and eating a home-cooked, locally sourced meal instead of grabbing fast food and heading to the mall for some recreational shopping. That simple choice not only prioritizes those we love by feeding them better food and spending time together, it also supports local farmers and saves energy as well. However, just as with choosing a slower life pace, choosing to prioritize relationships puts us in a position of swimming against the dominant cultural stream. It takes effort.

Prioritizing soulful self-care means setting aside time to look deeply at your own life, and honestly considering what makes you happy. This is an ongoing process of discovery, not a one-time activity accomplished over a weekend. It requires regular, ongoing introspection, a process not encouraged by society. It is the work of a lifetime. Step back. Take a time out. Breathe. Try to spend a few moments alone every day to reflect on your life, or a couple hours each week to simply be with your thoughts.

Not surprisingly, caring for the Earth can also be a process that lifts our spirits and mends our hearts. Psychotherapist Howard Clinebell calls this *ecobonding*—a process that heals and transforms not only our human lives but the Earth. Prioritizing your relationship with the natural world involves consciously spending time in natural surroundings, and allowing the Earth to become a sustaining, nurturing presence for you. It also means making lifestyle choices that help preserve and heal the Earth. This means different things to different people. The choices that are appropriate for you might not be so for others.

Practices

Cloud Watching On a sunny day, find a place with an unobstructed view of the sky. Spread out a blanket and spend at least a half hour daydreaming and staring at clouds. If you'd like, bring a picnic lunch. Be sure to unplug—no electronic devices of any sort are permitted while engaging in the serious business of cloud watching.

Small Change Adopt one new Earth-friendly habit. This can be something like hanging out your laundry on sunny days, or taking a ceramic mug to meetings instead of using the provided styrofoam cups. Make it simple, but make it stick. Don't choose something so difficult that you will quit after one or two times. Whenever you engage in your new habit, take a moment and pause to think about how you are connected to the Earth and all its systems.

Touchstone Connections For a week, try this experiment. Place a small object, such as a polished stone or seashell, into your pocket or change purse every day. Whenever you reach into your pocket or purse and see or touch the object, ask yourself the simple question: What does my soul need at this point in my life? Allow yourself to sit with the question for a week, and allow the object to be the gentle reminder to focus. After the week is up, take some time to reflect in your journal on the answers that emerged.

Large Group—Downsizing Potlatch This is an event that takes the ordinary yard sale to a whole new level. Have group members donate items that they no longer need or want, and offer them free to the wider community. (You may want to offer them to group members first. You never know what someone might be able to use.) Advertise the event however you like. You can set limits for a certain number of items per person or you can let people decide their own limits. If you wish, set up a donation jar for a designated eco-charity. You can offer free information on eco-friendly, simple living, or you can pass out free cookies. The point is to hold an event that has an entirely different tone than an ordinary sale. Tap into your group's innate creativity, and let the potlatch reflect your values in a unique and beautiful way.

For Reflection

⤳   What is your psychological or spiritual equivalent of junk food? Does it adequately meet your needs or not?

⤳   What is your favorite place in nature? Why is it your favorite?

⤳   How can you make lifestyle changes that help create space and time for meeting your soul's needs? What needs to change? What is fine as it is?

⤳   What makes you truly and deeply happy? Can you make more room in your life for this?

TWENTY-THREE

Widening Our Circle

Six degrees of separation. You've heard that one, haven't you? It's the theory that each person on Earth is connected by six steps or fewer to every other person on the planet. The theory may or may not be true for every single person—it's impossible to know for sure. But the idea that we are all interconnected more closely than any of us had imagined is absolutely true, though perhaps in ways that the theory doesn't consider. In fact, our entire global biosphere, including humans, is interconnected in ways that we are just beginning to understand. J.E. Lovelock's Gaia hypothesis, first proposed more than thirty years ago, considers the entire Earth as one integrated, self-regulating, living organism. It has gradually gained acceptance as an ecological paradigm for the twenty-first century and beyond. According to the Gaia hypothesis, what we do to one part of the Earth, we do to the entire Earth. What we do to the Earth, we do to ourselves.

Indigenous peoples are far ahead of industrialized cultures in realizing this truth. David Suzuki and Peter Knudtson describe the view of the Amazonian Desana people, who see themselves as embedded within an unceasing energy flow. In *Wisdom of the Elders*, they write,

> When a Desana elder looks out upon the sacred circuit of sunlight that oozes slowly through the vast rain forest that engulfs him and his community, he sees inherent to this system a mandate to human beings to "borrow" no more than they absolutely require from these precious, primal flows and to give back to the great system, through prayer and practice, gifts comparable to what they have been given.

Imagine a world where this ethic is translated into our own culture and becomes the norm.

We are deeply interconnected. Drought in Africa churns up dust into the atmosphere. The dust travels across the Atlantic, and affects cloud formation over the Caribbean. A man orders a burger in a fast food restaurant. The burger, shipped from South America, came from a cow raised on land that was formerly part of the Amazon rainforest, now burned and cleared for grazing. An empty plastic bag floats across a parking lot next to a suburban big box store in the U.S., and ends up floating in the middle of the Pacific six months later.

But there are other ways of being connected as well: A woman purchases a bag of fair trade coffee at her local co-op. Somewhere in Sumatra a father buys school books for his children with money earned from his small family coffee plantation. A teenager, after learning of the crisis in the rainforest, decides to skip the trip to the burger place and packs a lunch instead. A couple serves locally grown food at their wedding reception, supporting the farmers of their foodshed in the process. A retired man spends a Saturday morning cleaning up a stream with a conservation group, ensuring that hundreds of pieces of plastic will never make it to the ocean.

As the Desana elder so wisely recognized, we too are embedded within larger systems, upon which we depend for our very lives. Trees take in carbon dioxide and give off oxygen. Water evaporates, and then falls as rain. Cycles of ocean currents keep northern Europe warmer than latitudes alone would allow. Soil bacteria break down dead plant matter, making nutrients available for new growth. Fungi break down environmental toxins. Even the planet Jupiter plays a role. Its gravity helps deflect asteroids that might otherwise bombard our planet into a lifeless rock. Not only are we a part of larger systems, we ourselves are a system. Each of us exists in symbiotic relationship with millions of helpful bacteria that digest our food and in so doing make our survival possible.

We really are connected, like it or not. No one is an island. Moving forward toward creating truly sustainable societies in the twenty-first century requires that we not only acknowledge but embrace that fact. The choices we make ripple out from us like a pond ripples after a stone is tossed into it and have implications far beyond our immediate community. The great challenge of our still-new century is figuring out those implications, and changing the way we relate to the world based on what we learn.

Practices

Degrees of Gratitude Sit comfortably, and recall a meal you ate recently. Offer thanks for the people, animals, plants, and Earth systems that interacted to bring that meal to you. For example, if you ate a cheese sandwich, give thanks for the person who made the sandwich, the cashier who sold you the bread and cheese, the dairy clerk, the baker, the workers at the cheese factory, the person who drove the milk truck from the farm, the farmer, the cow, the hay and the pasture that fed the cow, the sun for making the grass grow in the pasture, the flour mill, the wheat field, the soil in which the wheat grew, and the rain that fell on the field. You might even offer thanks for the evolutionary process that brought into being cows and cheese-making bacteria, or the wild ancestor of cultivated wheat. This meditation can be as simple or as involved as you wish. It's a sort of spiritual cousin to the Buddhist tradition of loving-kindness, or metta, meditation.

Mindful Choices As our awareness of the environmental impact of our lifestyle grows, we naturally begin to change the way we live. In your journal, describe one major area of your life as a consumer. You might write about food, clothing, holidays, travel, driving habits, or whatever. After describing your habits, delve deeply into questioning why you do things the way you do. Then spend some time considering the obstacles that stand in the way of making changes. Be honest and gentle with yourself, acknowledging that while the spirit may be willing, change is not always easy in practice. Finally, brainstorm some do-able changes that could work for you. Do any of these have spiritual implications? If so, what?

How Wide Is Your Circle? Clear your altar space. Walk from room to room, and make a mental note of where the various objects in your home originated. Perhaps you have electronics from Japan, souvenirs from a Caribbean vacation, heirlooms from your family's country of origin, a fair trade knickknack from Africa, and some locally produced crafts. Choose several human-made items that originated from a variety of locales, and place these on your altar. As you do, think about the people who made these items, and what life might be, or might have been, like for them. What do you have in common? What is different? Leave the items in place for several days and allow yourself some time to muse on the interconnectedness of it all.

Large Group—Create Your Own Visualization Gather together and spend a little time discussing the idea of interconnectedness as it applies to people, animals, and Earth systems. Then, allow group members about twenty minutes alone to reflect on the many connections that exist in our world. Have them write a brief meditation or visualization that explores this theme. By now, participants have likely done several of the visualizations in this book, but if not, they can look back at earlier chapters for ideas on how to write one. After the alone time, gather again and have a few participants share their creations with the group if they are comfortable doing so. Discuss any new insights that may emerge.

For Reflection

∾   How is your life connected to the lives of those around you? What impact does your life have on others? What impact do they have on you?

∾   What might the phrase widening our circle mean in different contexts? Can you widen your circle and simplify your life at the same time?

∾   How are you connected both to people from your past and generations yet to come? How do choices and decisions ripple out over time?

∾   Imagine a society where our interconnectedness with the Earth was honored and celebrated. What would such a society look like?

TWENTY-FOUR

Falling in Love

The path of creation is joyful. Instead of dwelling on and being paralyzed by all the negativity of the world, we decide to create the type of world in which we want to live. This is a sacred place, where we walk on holy ground with every step and form deep and lasting relationships and communities where diversity is honored and uniqueness is respected, and where the Earth itself is healed and restored as much as possible. Sounds nice, doesn't it?

Probably many of us shake our heads at the impossibility of it all, and understandably so. All of us at some point have felt some despair at the state of things. In *My Name is Chellis, and I'm in Recovery from Western Civilization*, Chellis Glendinning puts it this way:

> We are powerless before the civilization we inhabit, and we are powerless over the destiny of our lives within this civilization. This statement does not mean that you and I are powerless as individuals. Indeed, we each have the power to heal our personal wounds, to band together with our neighbors to protest a specific technological

or political encroachment, to attempt to build human-scale community. What we are powerless over is the dysfunctional process that is so tightly clamped over our very personal and political choice.

True. But fortunately, this is not the end of the story. There are greater forces at work here, but just how they will affect us remains to be seen.

There is no doubt that we are in the midst of planetary change. We have now surpassed the limits of Earth's ability to regenerate its life-support systems. The climate is changing. Energy sources that fueled the Industrial Revolution may not last much longer. We are in the midst of a major transition, and the future doesn't seem as clearly predictable as it once did. In the end, we will create a sustainable way of life, one way or another. The question is how to get there.

The chances of a positive short- and long-term future are far greater if we begin creating it now. If we start making the changes we want to see—cultivating reverence and awe for the Earth and allowing that reverence to form the foundation for our way of being—we are on the way to recreating the Earth. Thoreau understood this when he wrote in *On Man & Nature*, "When I would recreate myself, I seek the darkest wood, the thickest and most interminable, and to the citizen, most dismal swamp. I enter the swamp as a sacred place—a *sanctum sanctorum*. There is the strength, the marrow of nature." This is the kind of strength that will sustain us through the necessary losses and changes to come.

Insects that undergo metamorphosis from a larva to their adult form enter a cocoon, where they are transformed. In the cocoon, the larva begins to dissolve. The old form collapses, and the new winged insect begins to form. The process is directed by so-called *imaginal* cells. These cells facilitate the transformation in ways that scientists are only beginning to understand. Our culture and our world are entering the cocoon. Change is upon us. Old ways are dissolving. Those who embark on the path of creation are the imaginal cells of this global process. We must envision the new, and midwife it into being through our dreams and our hard work. There is no other way.

The joyful part comes into play when we see just how much we love this exquisite, blue-green jewel that is our home. We are creatures of this place. We are the consciousness of Gaia, now able to realize this fact, truly understand it, and act upon it in ways that previous generations could not. We are the beloved children, the prodigal sons and daughters of our planet, who now understand the need to come home. We are the beloved children, now growing up, who realize that excess is unsustainable, greed is unacceptable, responsibility is a necessity, and our adulthood as a species is upon us. As mature beings now, we have fallen in love: utterly, madly, and gloriously in love with this place, this Earth and all who live upon it, human and non-human. We are head over heels for this sublime and unimaginable state of being. We are in love with Life, not our own small lives, but Life with a capital L. The Universe and All That Is. Life.

Ceremony of Closure Just as at the beginning, create a small personal ritual to mark the journey you have taken. Through words or actions, symbolize the Path of Awakening, the Path of Un-Learning, the Path of Discovery, and the Path of Creation. Incorporate elements of previous exercises, or create something entirely new.

Journal Closure Even if you plan to write more in your journal later, spend some time re-reading what you have written and reflect on your experience of working through the practices of this book. Which ones resonated strongly with you? Did you feel drawn to any particular ideas? What made you uncomfortable? Why?

Beloved Earth Go to your favorite outdoor place. It can be a park, nature trail, open space, or even your backyard. Anyplace is fine, as long as it's your favorite. Bring a gift of thanks and leave it somewhere nearby in an inconspicuous place where it is unlikely to be disturbed by people. Your gift can be a small token that symbolizes your gratitude and appreciation for the Earth. Make sure it's something natural, not synthetic—you don't want to litter. Consider these suggestions, or come up with one of your own: flowers, birdseed, bread, a seashell, a small stone, water, honey, a natural-fiber ribbon tied to a tree branch, a lock of your hair, dried herbs, cornmeal, beer, wine, or an object of unfinished wood. Keep it small. If it is a gift like birdseed or cornmeal, a handful is enough. Anything more permanent, like a shell or stone, should be small enough to be inconspicuous. It should blend in with the land. Offer your gift, and spend some time pondering what it means to love the Earth.

Large Group—Celebration of Life Mark the end of your group's journey together with a ceremonial celebration of life. Decorate your group altar with symbols of your love for the Earth and all its creatures. Share poetry, stories, and songs. Eat a meal together. Reflect on your experiences as a group, and share memories. Gather in circle, hold hands, and reflect on what it means to love the Earth. You might brainstorm future actions. Make your celebration reflect your group and its unique vision for the world. Honor that vision, and honor yourselves as participants in it.

For Reflection

∾   Have you ever had an experience that caused you to feel a sense of love for the natural world? What was it? How did it affect you?

∾   What does loving the Earth mean to you? What might it mean in a broader cultural context?

∾   Do you think a better future is possible? If so, how can we get there? If not, why not?

∾   What now? Where do you go from here?

Beyond the Paths—Finding Your Own Way

We're nearing the end of this particular journey together, but the journey of your lifetime and mine goes on. Together with all the myriad non-human life forms that share our home world, as well as our sister and brother humans, we live out our brief days embedded in Life's grander tale. The question we must now ask ourselves is, How shall we live? Once we begin to spiritually connect with the Earth, our source, what then?

Our answers will vary greatly from person to person. Some may choose to make radical changes in their lifestyles, perhaps switching careers or radically downsizing their consumption habits. Others may become outspoken advocates in the public arena. Some may step forward to lead community greening efforts. Many may not have the ability to make extreme changes, but instead will make a lot of small shifts in daily habits, with the sum total of them adding up to a different lifestyle entirely. It's all good, and it's all necessary, and it adds up to what environmental writer Bill McKibben calls the "durable future." So, let's get busy on all fronts. No excuses. Find your niche, your issue, your passion and get to work.

The Earth has already been radically changed by human activity, and these changes will continue into the immediate and distant future regardless of our actions now. If, all of a sudden, humanity was magically beamed off the planet, and the Earth was left to heal unimpeded, global warming would continue for decades to come, invasive species would keep invading, and other species would go extinct. Eventually the disrupted systems would slowly balance out into a new dynamic equilibrium, as the remaining species rebounded and pollution levels declined. Evolution would continue as always, creating new species from the ones that remain and recreating biodiversity over millions of years. This does not mean that all our efforts are in vain. On the contrary, since we obviously cannot beam ourselves off to planet Utopia, we must do our utmost to restore the Earth, and this is at its heart a spiritual task.

In the process of becoming civilized, we have denied, silenced, and nearly destroyed our wild souls within. Our path to wholeness, and the restoration of the Earth, requires that we awaken this part of ourselves, and allow it to grow and ultimately to thrive. We need to "un-civilize" our hearts, and feel joy and awe at the miracle of our own existence, and the greater miracle of life itself. Thomas Berry writes that indigenous wisdom is characterized by an intimacy with the natural world. In our process of un-civilizing, we must recreate this indigenous wisdom within each of us, not to co-opt any existing indigenous culture, but to rediscover its essence, which is a part of our human legacy. We must reclaim the Holy Ground. We must re-sanctify the Earth. When our culture finally does this, the solutions for the physical problems will follow, since care for the Earth will be the norm for our behavior, not an aberration.

This doesn't mean we all will become tree-hugging Druids, dancing under the moon. While I have nothing against Druids and dancing under the moon is a lovely way to spend an evening, a more realistic possibility is that this natural form of spirituality can be expressed alongside of, or even integrated within, our present religious institutions. Whether we call it *creation care*, *eco-spirituality*, or *deep green religion* matters less than tangibly reconnecting with the Earth. Natural spirituality is not contingent on any particular religious belief, and it does not require us to abandon our beloved traditions, beliefs, or faith. Instead, we can integrate this kind of spirituality into, or practice it alongside, our traditions. For those who hold no particular religious convictions, some form of natural spirituality can form the basis of a meaningful, life-enriching practice, unfettered by formal dogma.

There are many ways that this might this play out on a day-to-day basis. Think back on your experiences with the practices in this book. Consider which types of practices you felt most drawn to. If altar work resonated with you, think about how you might incorporate more of that into your ongoing spiritual life. You might design several altars, both inside your home and out, and spend time in quiet contemplation with them. You could repeat your favorite visualizations on a regular basis, and create more of your own. Artists could incorporate the theme of sacred Earth into their work. If the group service projects struck a chord, consider making some sort of purposeful activity a central focus of your spiritual practice. Engaging in activism in an intentional, mindful way can move it beyond the purely physical realm, as well as guard against burnout. For example, if you decide to work in your community to advocate for cleaning up a toxic waste site, you can incorporate a short ritual of intention before you head out the door. Alternatively, you might meditate or pray near the site. The point is to engage your spirit, not just your mind or hands.

The trick is to balance working for environmental progress and Earth healing with nurturing your own spirit. For example, as important as it is to support local, sustainable agriculture, it is equally important to feed your soul along with your body. Healing your own personal disconnect with the

Earth is the foundation for all other positive changes, and the only path to creating a truly sustainable culture. And don't think that you aren't disconnected just because you might be living a more eco-friendly lifestyle than the next person. Simply by living in Western society (particularly American), you are virtually guaranteed to have been affected by that society to some degree. Spiritual practices like the ones in this book can help you step back a bit from the culture and see the dysfunctional paradigms upon which it rests. Once you are aware of the dysfunction, it becomes easier to spot in everyday life, and you will find yourself questioning the assumptions on which our collective bad habits rest.

It's also important to engage with nature in your local area. Your bioregion and local land base is your home. It is your direct line to Mama Gaia, even as it is also a part of you. Whether it is a desert, prairie, city, or formerly wooded suburb, it is your Sacred Space and Holy Ground. Engage with it, interact with it. Get to know it through the seasons and over time. Let it sustain you, even as you work to sustain it.

Finally, there are selfish reasons for cultivating a nature-focused spirituality. Simply put, spiritually healthy people who are in touch with the natural world are physically and mentally healthy as well. Humans evolved in close communion with the natural world. Indigenous cultures know this, and live it. They enjoy a level of inner peace and psychological health that is virtually unknown to fast-paced, stressed-out Westerners. When we step back and examine our lives, rethink our consumerist priorities and re-engage with the natural world, we find healing for our bodies, minds, relationships, and spirits. We discover a level of wholeness in our inmost self that we had not realized was possible. We step out with joy, walking the sacred paths of our beloved home.

We smile, and Earth smiles along with us. Both of us have begun to heal.

Tips for Group Facilitators

Just as every individual is unique, so is every group. Different personalities, meeting spaces, group sizes, and ages of participants all impact the unique character of a gathering. The practices here are very adaptable and I encourage you to adopt a flexible approach and make whatever changes you think might help your group get the most from the material.

It is best for each participant to have his or her own copy of the book to use between sessions. If cost is a barrier for some participants, consider purchasing a few copies from donated funds and offering them for free to those who need them. Brainstorm ways to keep this as anonymous as possible given your situation.

Ideally, session length should range from one and a half to two hours. This allows for plenty of time for the group to gather, do a practice or two, and discuss some of the questions at the end of the chapter. Practices vary considerably in the time it takes to complete them. Some will take only a few minutes, while others may take an hour or more. It is helpful for the facilitator to plan accordingly and estimate the time needed for the group to complete a practice based on the size and nature of the group. If time is short at the end of a session, prioritize the group discussion questions based on the interests of the group. Also, consider conducting a simple opening and closing ceremony—such as holding hands in a circle and reading a prayer or quotation—to provide a clear beginning and ending to the session.

Although any sized group can utilize the large group practices, very large groups (over a hundred) may find it helpful to split into groups of twenty-five or fewer for practices that involve lots of discussion. Other practices, such as the hunger banquet described in chapter six, work well in very large groups. Your meeting space may also affect how your group interacts. For example, it can be challenging to lead discussions in a church sanctuary setting that is laid out in the typical pulpit-pew pattern. Also, when working with very large groups in large spaces, consider the acoustics. Can everyone hear when others speak? Do you need to use a sound system?

When using altars in a large space, consider the size of the items on the altar in relation to the overall space. If they are too small to be seen, consider using several smaller altars placed strategically throughout the area. The altar work described in this book is mostly personal and small-scale. Plan for how it can be scaled-up for use in a larger space. Tap into your creativity and find or invent a solution that works for your group and your meeting place.

It may be helpful to use a whiteboard or newsprint to write down ideas during group discussions. Participants may also want to supplement their solo journal entries by using their journals to write down thoughts during group or pair/triad sessions. This should be up to the individual. Some people are very language oriented—writing down every thought comes naturally to them. Others may feel that this much writing intrudes on the flow of their experience, and choose not to do so.

Finally, as any group facilitator knows, there are many personalities present within a given group. It is your job as facilitator to encourage participation without demanding public speaking from very shy members. It is also important to prevent a few people from dominating the discussion. Consider establishing some simple parameters at the start. Participants can brainstorm some guidelines—such as not interrupting or engaging in side conversations—to help get the sessions started on a positive note. Even with guidelines, there may be times when you as a facilitator need to step in and bring the group back on track. Don't be afraid to be assertive if needed, while still being respectful of all. Enjoy!

Alphabetical List of Practices

Large Group Practices

For Further Exploration

Barlow, Connie. *Green Space, Green Time.* New York: Springer-Verlag, 1997.

Berry, Thomas. *The Dream of the Earth.* 2nd Ed. San Franciso, CA: Sierra Club Books, 2006.

————. *The Great Work: Our Way into the Future.* New York: Random House, 1999.

Berry, Wendell. *Collected Poems, 1957-1982.* New York: North Point Press, 1987.

Campbell, Joseph. *The Hero with a Thousand Faces.* 3rd Ed. Novato, CA: New World Library, 2008.

Carson, Rachel. *Silent Spring*, 40th Anniversary Ed. New York: Houghton Mifflin, 2002.

Clinebell, Howard. *Ecotherapy: Healing Ourselves, Healing the Earth.* Minneapolis, MN: Augsburg Fortress, 1996.

Dawkins, Richard. *The Ancestor's Tale: A Pilgrimage to the Dawn of Evolution.* New York: Houghton Mifflin, 2004.

Dowd, Michael. *Thank God for Evolution: How the Marriage of Science and Religion Will Transform Your Life and Our World.* New York: Penguin, 2008.

Fiand, Barbara. *Awe-Filled Wonder: The Interface of Science and Spirituality.* New York: Paulist Press, 2008.

Fitzgerald, Waverly. *Slow Time: Recovering the Natural Rhythm of Life.* 2nd Ed. Priestess of Swords Press, 2007.

Glendinning, Chellis. *My Name is Chellis, and I'm in Recovery from Western Civilization.* Gabriola Island, BC: New Catalyst Books, 1994.

Goodenough, Ursula. *The Sacred Depths of Nature.* Oxford: Oxford University Press, 1998.

Griffin, Susan. *Woman and Nature: The Roaring Inside Her.* Sierra Club Books, 2000.

Hawking, Stephen. *A Brief History of Time.* New York: Bantam, 1996.

Jensen, Derrick. *Endgame, Volume 1: The Problem of Civilization.* New York: Seven Stories Press, 2006.

———. *Endgame, Volume 2: Resistance.* New York: Seven Stories Press, 2006.

Kindersly, Anabel and Barnabas. *Children Just Like Me.* New York: DK Publishing, 1995.

Korton, David C. *Agenda for a New Economy: From Phantom Wealth to Real Wealth.* San Francisco: Berrett-Koehler, 2009.

———. *The Great Turning: From Empire to Earth Community.* San Francisco: Berrett-Koehler, 2006.

Kunstler, James Howard. *The Long Emergency: Surviving the End of Oil, Climate Change and Other Converging Catastrophes of the Twenty-First Century.* New York: Atlantic Monthly Press, 2005.

Lovelock, J.E. *Gaia: A New Look at Life on Earth.* Oxford: Oxford University Press, 2000.

Macy, Joanna. *Coming Back to Life: Practices to Reconnect Our Lives, Our World*. Gabriola Island, BC: New Society Publishers, 1998.

McElroy, Susan Chernak. *Why Buffalo Dance: Animal and Wilderness Meditations Through the Seasons*. Novato, CA: New World Library, 2006.

McKibbon, Bill. *Deep Economy: The Wealth of Communities and the Durable Future*. Oxford: Oneworld Publications, 2007.

———. *Eaarth: Making a Life on a Tough New Planet*. New York: Times Books, 2010.

———. *The End of Nature*. New York: Random House, 2006.

Menzel, Peter, Charles C. Mann and Paul Kennedy. *Material World: A Global Family Portrait*. San Francisco, CA: Sierra Club Books, 1995.

Monbiot, George. *Heat: How to Stop the Planet from Burning*. Cambridge, MA: South End Press, 2009.

Norris, Gunilla. *Being Home: Discovering the Spiritual in the Everyday*. Mahwah, NJ: Paulist Press, 2001.

Oliver, Mary. *Why I Wake Early: New Poems*. Boston: Beacon Press, 2005.

Roberts, Elizabeth, Ed. *Earth Prayers From Around the World: 365 Prayers, Poems, and Invocations for Honoring the Earth*. New York: HarperCollins, 1993.

Quinn, Daniel. *Ishmael: An Adventure of the Mind and Spirit*. New York: Bantam Books, 1995.

Sagan, Carl. *Contact*. New York: Simon & Schuster, 1986.

Schumacher, E.F. *Small Is Beautiful: Economics as if People Mattered*. New York: Harper & Row, 1989.

Seidel, Peter. *Invisible Walls: Why We Ignore the Damage We Inflict on the Planet . . . and Ourselves*. Amherst, NY: Prometheus Books, 2001.

Suzuki, David. *The Big Picture: Reflections on Science, Humanity, and a Quickly Changing Planet*. Vancouver, BC: Greystone Books, 2009.

Suzuki, David and Peter Knudtson. *Wisdom of the Elders: Honoring Sacred Native Visions of Nature*. New York: Bantam, 1992.

Swimme, Brian and Thomas Berry. *The Universe Story: From the Primordial Flaring Forth to the Ecozoic Era—A Celebration of the Unfolding of the Cosmos*. New York: HarperCollins, 1994.

Thoreau, Henry D. *On Man & Nature*. Mt. Vernon, NY: Peter Pauper Press, 1960.

———. *Walden*. Boston: Beacon Press, 2004.

Wells, Spencer. *Deep Ancestry: Inside the Genographic Project*. Washington, D.C.: National Geographic, 2007.

Wolff, Robert. *Original Wisdom: Stories of an Ancient Way of Knowing*. Rochester, VT: Inner Traditions, 2001.

Film

A Crude Awakening—The Oil Crash, 2007

An Inconvenient Truth, 2006

Evolution, PBS, 2002

Life, Discovery Channel Video, 2009

Origins: Nova, 2004

Planet Earth: The Complete Collection, BBC Video, 2007

The 11th Hour, 2007

The End of Suburbia: Oil Depletion and the Collapse of the American Dream, 2007

The Corporation, 2004

Online

Alternatives for Simple Living: www.simpleliving.org
American Institute of Philanthropy: www.charitywatch.org
Global Footprint Network: www.footprintnetwork.org
Grist (Environmental News): www.grist.org
Oxfam America: www.oxfamamerica.org
Oxford Ancestors: www.oxfordancestors.com
Poor Will's Almanack: www.poorwillsalmanack.com
The Daily Climate: www.dailyclimate.org
The Genographic Project: https://genographic.nationalgeographic.com/
    genographic/index.html
The Great Story: www.thegreatstory.org
Living on Earth: www.loe.org
Planet Harmony: www.myplanetharmony.com
What Is Missing?: www.whatismissing.net

Music

Peter Mayer Sings the Great Story, available from www.petermayer.net

Acknowledgments

I would like to offer special thanks to the many wonderful people who have helped bring this book to completion. I truly could not have done it without all of you. First, thanks to Judy Torgas, who edited the book proposal in the very early stages, and offered many helpful suggestions that got this project off the ground from the start.

Thanks to the people at Skinner House who decided to take a chance on me as a first-time author. Thanks to my editor, Mary Benard, whose insightful suggestions have made this a better book than it would have otherwise been. Thank you to Marshall Hawkins for his copyediting expertise and for shepherding the book to completion. Big thanks to Darry Madden, who brought creativity and enthusiasm to the marketing process. Thanks also to Design Director Suzanne Morgan, Publishing Manager Joni McDonald, and Production Assistant Kate Bates for all their hard work. Special thanks to Skinner House Administrator Betsy Martin, who sent me one of the best emails I've ever received, telling me that my proposal was accepted.

Thanks also go out to my circle sisters, both local and virtual, for their unceasing affirmation and friendship. Thank you for believing in me. Finally to my friends and family, especially my husband Patrick, thank you for your love and support over the years.